Born of Imagination: The Dance of the Dreamers

aarat

Published by aarat, 2024.

BORN OF IMAGINATION: THE DANCE OF THE DREAMERS

First edition. November 15, 2024.

ISBN: 979-8230154761

Written by aarat.

Preface

The story you are about to embark on is not just a tale of creation and existence; it is an exploration of the **infinite**"of the rhythms that guide our souls and the threads that bind us to the fabric of the universe. Within these pages lies a journey into the heart of a cosmic spiral, where light and darkness, sound and silence, motion and stillness, all intertwine in a dance as eternal as time itself.

At its core, this story reflects a timeless truth: that life is not a destination but a journey, an unfolding of infinite possibilities. The dreamers of this tale, with their sparks of light and their steps of creation, are not merely character"they are reflections of us all. They embody our longing to create, our desire to understand, and our need to connect with something greater than ourselves.

The spiral they traverse is both a world unto itself and a metaphor for the cycles of existence that we all experience. It invites us to question the boundaries of what we know and challenges us to embrace the unknown. Through their journey, the dreamers uncover a truth that resonates deeply: the infinite is not a place we reach, but a state of being we awaken to.

This story is for the seeker" the ones who long to dance beyond the confines of their world, to create, to dream, and to discover the beauty of becoming. It is for those who look into the void and see not emptiness, but infinite potential.

May the rhythm of the spiral echo in your heart, and may its light guide you on your own journey into the infinite.

Let the dance begin.

In a peaceful countryside, where the golden sun kissed fields of green, there lived a wise old hen named Clara. She was the matron of a bustling barnyard, known for her stories and the strange, sparkling egg she always carried close.

The Special Egg

This egg wasn't ordinary—it shimmered faintly under the sunlight, as though it held a secret within. The younger hens often whispered about it, and the chicks pecked curiously around, but Clara never revealed its origin.

One day, a curious young chick named Pip mustered the courage to ask, "Grandmother Clara, why do you always carry that egg? What's so special about it?"

Clara clucked softly, her eyes warm with affection. "This egg," she began, "reminds me of a question that has puzzled the world for ages. Do you know what it is?"

Pip tilted his head. "What question?"

"Which came first," Clara said with a smile, "the chicken or the egg?"

The Story of Origins

The barnyard animals gathered around as Clara began her tale.

"A long time ago, when the world was still new, there was a great debate among the creatures of the earth. The Creator, in their infinite wisdom, sought to teach the world an important lesson about beginnings and growth.

"They created the Egg, fragile yet full of promise, and placed it in the warm embrace of the Hen. 'The egg carries the potential for life,' the Creator said, 'but the hen nurtures it, protects it, and brings it into being.'

"The animals marveled at the wisdom of the Creator's plan. From then on, they learned that beginnings don't matter as much as what we do with what we have. The egg and the hen became partners, each essential to the other. And so the world grew, cycle upon cycle, with no need to answer which came first."

A Lesson for All

Pip stared at the shimmering egg, understanding dawning in his young eyes. "So it's not about who comes first," he chirped, "but about how we care for each other?"

Clara nodded. "Exactly, little one. Life is about connection, not competition. We each play our part, and together, we make the world whole."

From that day, Pip carried Clara's lesson in his heart. And as he grew into a strong rooster, he passed on the wisdom of the egg and the hen, ensuring the barnyard thrived with harmony and care.

The shimmering egg? It remained a mystery, but its message lived on forever.

The Day of the Egg's Secret

Years passed, and Clara grew older. Pip, now a proud rooster, often reflected on the wisdom she had shared. But the shimmering egg remained at the center of barnyard curiosity.

One sunny morning, Clara gathered all the animals. "Friends," she began, her voice steady but tinged with age, "it is time to reveal the secret of this egg. Its journey is near its end, and its story will soon become yours to carry forward."

The barnyard fell silent, each animal eager to witness the moment. Clara gently placed the egg on a soft bed of hay. The egg glimmered as if responding to her touch.

The Hatching

Suddenly, a faint crack echoed through the air. The shimmering egg began to tremble. The animals held their breath as tiny fissures spread across its delicate surface. Slowly, a small, glowing chick emerged, its down a radiant gold that seemed to reflect the sunlight.

The barnyard erupted in gasps of wonder. Clara's eyes sparkled with joy. "This," she said, "is the Heart of Life. The shimmering egg was a gift from the Creator, a reminder of the infinite potential within each of us. This chick represents hope, growth, and the beauty of nurturing life."

A Legacy of Care

The glowing chick, named Lumina by the animals, quickly became a symbol of unity and care in the barnyard. Under Clara's guidance, the animals worked together to ensure Lumina thrived. They realized that the egg's secret wasn't just about its beauty or mystery—it was about the collective effort to nurture and protect what matters most.

As Clara's days drew to a close, she passed the mantle of wisdom to Pip. "Remember," she said, "life is not a question of beginnings or endings. It is a continuous circle, with each of us playing our part. Cherish it, nurture it, and the cycle will never break."

A New Era

When Clara was gone, Lumina continued to grow, her golden feathers becoming a beacon for all. The barnyard thrived under Pip's leadership, filled with the spirit of unity and the timeless lesson of the egg and the hen.

And so, the story lived on—a tale passed from beak to beak, wing to wing, reminding all that success lies not in being first, but in working together to create something extraordinary.

Lumina's Gift

As Lumina matured, her golden feathers seemed to radiate even more brightly, lighting up the barnyard even during the darkest nights. Her presence became a source of inspiration, reminding every creature of the wisdom Clara had imparted. But Lumina herself often wondered what her true purpose was.

One evening, as the barnyard basked in the cool glow of the moon, Lumina approached Pip. "Father Pip," she said softly, "Clara always spoke of nurturing life and keeping the cycle unbroken. But what is my role in it?"

Pip, now a wise and seasoned leader, smiled warmly. "Lumina, you are a symbol of what we can achieve when we work together. But your purpose is yours to discover. Listen to your heart, and it will guide you."

The Great Storm

Not long after, a fierce storm descended upon the countryside. The wind howled, the rain lashed, and the barn trembled under nature's fury. The animals huddled together in fear, unsure if their shelter would hold.

As the storm raged, a frightened sparrow flew into the barn, soaked and shivering. "The river is rising," the sparrow chirped desperately. "The nests near the fields will be swept away!"

The barnyard erupted in panic, but Lumina stepped forward, her golden feathers glinting even in the dim light. "We must act quickly," she declared. "If we work together, we can save them!"

A Heroic Effort

Under Lumina's leadership, the animals sprang into action. The stronger animals formed a barrier with hay and wood to redirect the rising water, while the smaller ones helped the sparrows and other field animals move to higher ground.

Lumina herself waded into the floodwaters, guiding stragglers to safety. Her golden feathers became a beacon in the chaos, helping frightened creatures find their way.

When the storm finally subsided, the barnyard was left muddy and battered but intact. Thanks to Lumina's courage and the collective effort of the animals, not a single life was lost.

A New Dawn

As the sun rose the next morning, its light seemed to dance off Lumina's feathers, making her glow even brighter. The animals gathered around her, filled with gratitude and admiration.

Pip stepped forward, his eyes shining with pride. "Clara was right," he said. "Life is a continuous circle, and each of us plays a part. Lumina, you've shown us that true leadership comes from compassion and courage. You've fulfilled your purpose by uniting us and protecting the cycle of life."

A Legacy Reborn

From that day on, Lumina became the heart of the barnyard, embodying the wisdom of the egg and the hen. Her story, like Clara's, was passed down through generations, reminding all that success is not measured by what we gain for ourselves but by what we do for others.

And so, the barnyard thrived, its creatures bound together by the light of one golden hen and the timeless lesson she carried in her feathers: that life, in all its forms, is a gift meant to be nurtured, cherished, and shared.

The Journey Beyond

As seasons changed and years rolled on, Lumina grew into a majestic hen, her golden feathers becoming a symbol of hope not just for the barnyard but for the entire countryside. Word of her courage and wisdom spread far and wide, drawing animals from distant lands who came seeking her guidance.

One day, a weary tortoise arrived at the barnyard, carrying tales of a distant valley plagued by drought. "The crops have withered," he said, his voice heavy with despair. "The rivers have dried, and the animals are starving. We need someone with the light of hope to guide us."

Lumina felt a deep calling in her heart. "The barnyard has thrived because of unity and care," she said. "It's time to share that spirit with others. I will journey to the valley and help."

A Farewell and a Promise

The barnyard animals were reluctant to let Lumina go, but they understood the importance of her mission. Pip, though proud, felt a pang of sadness. "You've grown into everything Clara dreamed of," he said. "Remember, Lumina, wherever you go, the lessons of the egg and the hen will guide you."

Lumina promised to return one day, carrying the stories and successes of her journey. With the barnyard's blessings, she spread her golden wings and set off toward the parched valley, the sun casting a radiant glow around her.

Transforming the Valley

When Lumina arrived at the valley, she found a barren land where hope had all but disappeared. The animals were weak and divided, each struggling to survive alone.

Lumina gathered them together and shared the lessons she had learned from Clara and Pip: that life thrives through unity and care. She taught them to work together—digging canals to redirect water, planting drought-resistant crops, and building shelters to protect against the harsh sun.

Slowly but surely, the valley began to heal. The first trickles of water returned to the rivers, and green shoots emerged from the cracked soil. The animals, once isolated, now worked side by side, their spirits lifted by Lumina's golden light and unwavering determination.

The Cycle Continues

Years later, Lumina returned to the barnyard, her feathers still glowing but now carrying the stories of countless lives she had touched. She found the barnyard flourishing under Pip's continued leadership, its animals stronger and wiser.

As she stood in the familiar warmth of her home, Lumina realized that her journey was not an ending but another step in the endless cycle of growth and giving. She shared her tales with the barnyard, inspiring a new generation to carry forward the lessons of the egg and the hen.

A Legacy That Shines Forever

Lumina's story became a legend, passed down for generations across barnyards, valleys, and forests. Her golden feathers, now faded with age, remained a treasured symbol of hope, compassion, and the boundless potential of working together.

And so, the egg and the hen's tale continued to thrive, a timeless reminder that success lies not in what we take, but in what we give—and in the light we leave behind for others to follow.

The Next Generation

As Lumina aged gracefully, she spent her days mentoring the younger animals in the barnyard. Her golden feathers, though now softened with time, still glimmered faintly, as if holding the essence of her lifelong journey.

One day, a peculiar egg appeared in the barnyard. It was unlike any other—speckled with silver and faintly glowing, much like the egg Clara had once carried. The animals whispered in awe, wondering if the egg was a sign of something extraordinary.

Lumina approached the egg with a knowing smile. "Every beginning carries a promise," she said, her voice soft yet full of wisdom. "This egg is a reminder that the cycle of life and growth is eternal. Just as I once emerged to guide and nurture, someone new will rise to carry forward the lessons we've all learned."

A Mysterious Hatchling

When the egg finally hatched, a small, silvery chick emerged, its feathers shimmering under the sun. The barnyard animals named her Nova, a star born to light up the future.

Nova, curious and full of energy, often followed Lumina around, eager to learn about the world. Lumina shared stories of Clara, Pip, and her own adventures, instilling in Nova the values of compassion, courage, and community.

"You are not just my successor," Lumina told Nova one evening as the sun set over the barnyard. "You are the continuation of a legacy. But your path will be your own to forge. Remember, success is not about shining the brightest—it's about lighting the way for others."

Nova's First Test

One winter, the barnyard faced an unexpected challenge. A deep frost settled over the land, threatening the food supply and the lives of the smaller animals. The barnyard animals, though experienced, found themselves unsure of how to respond to such an intense cold.

Nova, despite her youth, stepped forward. "We've learned so much from Lumina and those before her," she said. "Let's use what we know to protect each other."

Under Nova's guidance, the animals worked tirelessly. They dug through the snow to uncover buried seeds, used their combined warmth to shield the weakest among them, and rationed food carefully to ensure everyone survived.

The Passing of the Torch

When spring finally arrived, the barnyard celebrated their survival and unity. Lumina, watching from her favorite perch, felt a deep sense of fulfillment. Nova had proven herself not just as a leader but as the next bearer of the barnyard's legacy.

In her final days, Lumina gathered the animals around her. "The lessons of the egg and the hen have been passed down through generations," she said. "It is now Nova's time to lead, and your time to support her, just as you supported me."

A New Chapter

As Nova grew, she carried the wisdom of those who came before her, blending it with her own ideas and dreams. The barnyard flourished under her care, becoming a haven not just for its own animals but for those in need from far and wide.

Lumina's memory lived on, her golden feathers preserved in a special corner of the barnyard—a reminder of the endless cycle of life, love, and leadership.

And so, the story of the egg and the hen continued, with each new generation adding its own chapter, ensuring that the light of wisdom, compassion, and unity would never fade.

The Light Beyond the Barnyard

Under Nova's leadership, the barnyard became a place of innovation and growth. Animals from distant lands visited to learn the values of unity and compassion that had made the barnyard a beacon of hope. Nova's silvery feathers, now as luminous as Lumina's golden ones once were, symbolized the evolving legacy of the egg and the hen.

But Nova, ever curious, felt a pull to explore the world beyond the barnyard's borders. "The lessons we hold are powerful," she thought, "but how many more could benefit if we shared them farther?"

One crisp morning, Nova addressed the barnyard. "It's time for us to think beyond this place," she said. "We've created something beautiful here, but there are countless creatures out there who still struggle. Let's share what we've built with the world."

A Journey of Growth

Nova organized groups of animals to venture into nearby lands. Some carried seeds to barren fields, teaching others to farm and nurture the land. Others shared techniques for building strong shelters or conserving water. Everywhere they went, they spread the story of the egg and the hen, inspiring communities to work together.

Nova herself led a group to the mountains, where animals struggled to survive the harsh terrain. She taught them to create insulated shelters and forage for hidden resources. Her wisdom and guidance transformed their lives, and they, in turn, passed the knowledge to others.

The Return of the Egg

One day, while exploring a distant forest, Nova encountered an ancient tortoise who carried an egg unlike any she had ever seen. It glowed faintly with colors that seemed to shift with the light—gold, silver, and hints of deep blue.

"This egg," the tortoise explained, "is a symbol of beginnings yet unknown. It appears when a leader's journey is nearing its peak and a new era is about to dawn."

Nova brought the egg back to the barnyard, where it became a symbol of hope for future generations. The animals understood that their work was part of a larger cycle, and that the egg would one day hatch to begin a new chapter in their story.

The Eternal Legacy

As Nova grew older, she reflected on how far the barnyard's legacy had reached. The story of the egg and the hen was now known across valleys, mountains, and forests. Communities everywhere had adopted its lessons, creating networks of support and compassion that spanned great distances.

In her final days, Nova gathered the barnyard once more. "The egg represents the endless potential of life," she said. "Each of us is both the hen that nurtures and the egg that holds promise. Together, we ensure the cycle continues."

A New Beginning

When Nova passed, the mysterious egg she had brought home began to tremble. The barnyard animals gathered in awe as it hatched, revealing a chick with feathers that shimmered in all the colors of the rainbow. They named the chick Aura, a symbol of the unity and diversity that had come to define their way of life.

Aura grew up surrounded by the stories of Clara, Pip, Lumina, and Nova, carrying their wisdom while forging a new path. And so, the legacy of the egg and the hen lived on, a timeless tale of growth, unity, and the endless potential for a brighter future.

Aura's Vision

Aura, the radiant chick with rainbow-colored feathers, grew into a leader unlike any the barnyard had seen before. Her presence was mesmerizing, and her ability to connect with every creature—whether feathered, furred, or scaled—was unparalleled.

As she listened to the stories of those who had come before her, Aura began to notice something remarkable. Each leader had expanded the barnyard's reach, spreading its wisdom farther and farther. But she wondered, "What if we could bring all these scattered communities together? What if we could unite not just our barnyard, but the entire world?"

Aura envisioned a gathering—a great assembly where animals from every land would come together to share ideas, stories, and solutions to their common challenges. She called it the **Circle of Life Summit**.

Preparing for the Summit

Organizing the Circle of Life Summit was no small feat. Aura spent months sending messengers across valleys, mountains, and forests, inviting animals from every corner of the world. Each animal brought something unique: stories of resilience, tools for survival, and lessons learned from their struggles.

Back at the barnyard, the animals worked tirelessly to prepare for the summit. They built spaces for gatherings, prepared feasts from their abundant harvests, and even created maps to guide visitors to their home.

Aura's leadership was marked by collaboration. She empowered every animal, from the smallest mouse to the mightiest ox, to contribute their talents. "We are all part of the same circle," she reminded them. "Each of us has a role to play."

The Day of the Summit

The day of the Circle of Life Summit arrived, and animals from far and wide poured into the barnyard. Birds filled the skies with vibrant colors, their wings carrying tales of distant lands. Elephants from the savannah, foxes from the forest, and even fish carried in bowls by otters all gathered, their diverse voices blending in harmony.

Aura stood at the center of the assembly, her feathers shimmering in the sunlight. "Welcome, friends," she began. "Today, we celebrate not just our differences, but the unity that binds us. The lessons of the egg and the hen have taught us that life is a cycle, and each of us has the power to nurture it. Together, we can ensure a brighter future for all."

Sharing Knowledge

The summit became a melting pot of ideas and innovations. A flock of geese demonstrated how they navigated vast distances by working as a team, inspiring others to adopt similar strategies for cooperation. Forest animals taught water conservation techniques they had developed during droughts. In return, the barnyard animals shared their agricultural practices, helping others grow their own food.

The spirit of collaboration and mutual respect filled the air, and animals left the summit with new knowledge and friendships that would last lifetimes.

The Legacy Expands

As the summit ended, Aura realized her vision had only just begun. The barnyard was no longer just a home; it was now a hub of connection for creatures across the world. Communities that had once been isolated were now linked through a shared purpose: to nurture the cycle of life and support one another.

Before the visitors departed, Aura placed a shimmering egg at the center of the barnyard. "This egg," she declared, "represents the world we've built together. It will stay here as a reminder of what we've achieved and what we can continue to achieve when we work as one."

A New Chapter

Aura's rainbow feathers became a symbol of hope across the lands, and the Circle of Life Summit became an annual tradition. With each gathering, the bond between communities grew stronger, proving that the lessons of the egg and the hen could transcend boundaries and bring lasting change.

And so, the story of the egg and the hen continued, not just in the barnyard but across the world, carried forward by generations of animals united by a shared dream: a world where every life was nurtured, cherished, and celebrated as part of the infinite circle of existence.

The Ripple Effect

The annual **Circle of Life Summit** became a cornerstone for global unity. Each year, new faces arrived, and new ideas flowed through the barnyard. Animals from distant lands adapted the lessons of the egg and the hen to their own lives, creating self-sustaining communities that thrived on cooperation and mutual care.

Aura's barnyard was no longer just a place; it had become a symbol of hope and progress. Maps carried by migrating flocks marked the barnyard as "The Heart of Harmony," a destination for learning and collaboration.

A Challenge Arises

One year, during the preparations for the summit, messengers brought troubling news. A vast desert on the other side of the mountains had been struck by an unrelenting drought, and the animals there were on the brink of collapse. Despite their best efforts, the barren land could no longer sustain life.

Aura listened intently and then spoke with calm determination. "We cannot let despair take root," she said. "The barnyard began as a small haven, but its lessons have reached across the world. Now it's time to act on them. If the desert can no longer sustain life, we will bring life to the desert."

A Journey to the Desert

Aura led an expedition of animals to the arid lands. They carried seeds, tools, and knowledge from the barnyard. Engineers among them, like the beavers and moles, devised ways to redirect underground water to the surface. Birds carried seeds to scatter across the dry earth, while camels shared wisdom on surviving harsh climates.

For months, the animals worked tirelessly under the blazing sun. Aura, her rainbow feathers shimmering despite the heat, inspired them with her unwavering resolve. Slowly, patches of green began to appear, and small pools of water emerged where there had once been only cracked earth.

The Blooming Miracle

A year later, the once-barren desert had transformed into an oasis of life. Animals who had fled returned to their homeland, amazed at the miracle before them. They named the place **Aurora Fields**, in honor of Aura and her vision of unity and resilience.

The transformation of the desert became a beacon of possibility. It proved that no challenge was insurmountable when creatures worked together with purpose and care.

Passing the Torch

As Aura grew older, she knew her time as leader was nearing its end. She gathered the barnyard animals and representatives from all the lands connected through the Circle of Life.

"It is time for me to rest," she said, her voice steady and filled with love. "But the work we've begun must continue. Each of you is a leader, a nurturer, and a guardian of life. The egg and the hen's story doesn't belong to me—it belongs to all of us."

She turned to a young chick whose feathers gleamed with a soft, iridescent hue. The chick, named Solis, had shown wisdom and compassion beyond her years. Aura placed the ceremonial egg before Solis.

"This is yours to guard now," Aura said. "Carry it with the same love and hope that Clara, Lumina, Nova, and I have carried before you. Lead with your heart, and the world will follow."

A Legacy Without End

Aura's legacy lived on through Solis and the countless communities inspired by the barnyard's teachings. The Circle of Life Summit expanded, connecting even more distant lands. The lessons of the egg and the hen became eternal truths, whispered across generations and written in the winds that carried seeds of hope to every corner of the world.

And so, the story continued—an ever-evolving cycle of growth, love, and unity that turned even the harshest challenges into opportunities for flourishing life. The egg and the hen were no longer just symbols of a barnyard's wisdom—they were the heartbeat of a united and thriving world.

The Eternal Cycle

Years passed, and the world that had once been scattered and divided became a harmonious network of interwoven communities. The **Circle of Life Summit** continued to thrive, and its message of unity, resilience, and compassion spread like roots beneath the soil, connecting all living creatures.

Solis, now a wise and gentle leader, had become known far and wide as the *Heart of the Circle*. Her feathers, like the soft dawn, shimmered with warmth, and her presence brought peace to all who encountered her. Under her leadership, new generations of animals learned to not just survive, but to truly live in balance with nature and one another.

But even in such harmony, there were always new challenges, new territories to explore, and new lessons to be learned. The cycle of life continued, with each generation adding its own unique chapter to the never-ending story of the egg and the hen.

The Great Migration

One year, a vast migration began. It was not prompted by hunger or necessity but by a shared dream. Creatures from every land—birds, deer, foxes, elephants, and even marine life—felt a calling to journey to a distant mountain range known as **The Peaks of Light**, said to be a place where all life was said to be balanced in perfect harmony.

Solis, now in her elder years, knew the time had come to lead this migration. "We have brought life to so many places," she said to her people, "but now it is time to see where the world ends and begins. Let us find this place where all cycles meet."

The journey was long and arduous. The travelers encountered storms, deserts, and rugged terrain, but their determination was unyielding. Along the way, they helped one another, shared food, and supported the weaker among them. The lessons of the egg and the hen—of nurturing and community—guided them through every challenge.

The Peak of Light

After months of traveling, they reached the **Peaks of Light**, a high, misty plateau where the air was thin and the land shimmered with an ethereal glow. The mountain was a place of peace, its vast beauty overwhelming. But more than its beauty, it was the sense of connection that filled every creature who stepped onto its soil.

The Peak, it seemed, was a place where the cycles of the world converged. Here, the lessons of the egg and the hen were not just stories—they were the very fabric of life itself. The plants grew in perfect harmony, the rivers flowed gently, and every animal lived as one with the land.

It was here that Solis felt a deep understanding: the world was always in a state of becoming. The egg would always give birth to something new, and the hen would always nurture the next cycle. It was not a journey with a clear end but a journey that was its own reward—one that would continue for as long as the world spun.

A New Beginning

As the creatures stood together on the Peaks of Light, Solis felt a surge of hope and wonder. The journey had not only brought them closer to this sacred place but had deepened their understanding of the world they inhabited. They were all part of something far greater than themselves.

Solis looked out across the vast horizon, her heart filled with gratitude for the legacy that had been passed down to her—and for the legacy she would leave behind. She knew that the egg, in all its infinite possibilities, would always hold the promise of something new. And that the hen, in all its nurturing grace, would always guide the way forward.

With a serene smile, Solis spoke to the gathered animals. "The world is vast, and the cycle of life never ends. We are all part of this great circle, and each of us has the power to create, to nurture, and to pass forward the wisdom of the egg and the hen."

The Circle Lives On

As the animals settled on the Peaks of Light, they knew that their legacy, born from a humble barnyard, had rippled across the world in ways they could never fully comprehend. The story of the egg and the hen had become not just a tale but the foundation of a world built on compassion, unity, and life's endless potential.

And so, the circle continued, generation after generation. The egg and the hen's story would never end. It would live in every sunrise, in every heartbeat, in every new beginning and every nurturing hand. The legacy would endure forever, as eternal as life itself.

The Whisper of the Wind

Centuries passed, and the story of the egg and the hen had woven itself into the very fabric of the world's history. The barnyard that had once been a small, humble place was now a legend, a symbol of the interconnectedness of all life. The **Circle of Life Summit** had grown into a global gathering, and the lessons passed down through generations had shaped entire civilizations.

Yet, the world had not remained static. There were new challenges to face—shifting climates, evolving ecosystems, and the constant need to adapt to change. Even as the world flourished, the cycle of life had to be continually nurtured and protected. The wisdom of the egg and the hen had taken root in every community, but the world was vast, and the future uncertain.

The **Peaks of Light**, once a place of serene beauty and balance, now held a deeper significance. It became a sanctuary where leaders from all corners of the world came to reflect on the lessons of the past and renew their commitment to the endless cycle of life. It was there that the greatest leaders gathered to reflect on their journeys and pass on their wisdom.

The Seed of Change

One day, as the sun rose over the Peaks of Light, a soft wind whispered through the mountain, carrying with it the faintest scent of something new—something unlike anything the world had known. It was a seed, carried by the wind, a symbol of yet another beginning. This seed, however, was not like the seeds of plants or creatures of the earth. It was a **seed of possibility**, a force for transformation that had the potential to shape the world in ways unseen.

The elders of the summit gathered around the seed, drawn to it with a sense of quiet reverence. Among them was **Astra**, the newest leader to rise from the legacy of the egg and the hen. Astra, a creature born under the light of a thousand stars, had seen the world evolve and had helped shape it, but she knew that true growth required more than just reflection on the past—it required courage to look ahead.

The Gift of the Seed

Astra stood before the seed, feeling the weight of responsibility upon her. The world had come so far, but the future was always in motion, constantly evolving. "This seed," Astra thought, "is not just a symbol of the past, but a promise for the future."

With great care, Astra planted the seed in the sacred soil of the Peaks of Light. As she did, the winds began to swirl, and a brilliant light emanated from the ground, spreading outwards like the roots of a mighty tree. The seed began to grow, not into a single tree, but into a **network of life**, stretching across the globe. Its roots branched out, reaching into every community, every heart, and every corner of the earth.

The world had changed once again, as it always did. This new life was not just a continuation of the old—it was something more. It was a **new cycle**, a new chapter that would intertwine with all that had come before it, blending the wisdom of the past with the promise of the future.

A New Era

As the roots of the new tree of life spread, communities began to notice a shift. The world seemed to hum with new energy, with an awakening that resonated deeply within every creature. The trees bore fruit like never before, the rivers ran with clearer waters, and the earth felt more vibrant than it had in centuries. Astra, now standing tall in the light of a new dawn, realized that the world was once again on the brink of something extraordinary.

The old barnyard, where the first egg had been laid, had long since transformed into a sanctuary where creatures from all walks of life came to remember the lessons passed down through the ages. Now, it was no longer just a place—it was a **living story**, a symbol of the interconnectedness that had made the world thrive.

Astra stood before the ever-growing tree of life, its branches stretching far and wide, and with a deep breath, she spoke to the gathered animals and leaders: "The egg, the hen, the seed—these are not mere stories. They are our legacy, our future, and our purpose. As long as the earth spins, the cycles will continue. Our role is not just to protect life but to continue to evolve with it, to guide it as it transforms and grows."

The Cycle Continues

And so, the world once again embraced the endless cycle of life. The egg and the hen had laid the foundation for a world where every generation's story was not just a chapter, but a vital thread in a tapestry of growth, resilience, and renewal. The new seed, planted by Astra, would continue to grow, its roots entwining with the wisdom of all those who had come before.

The winds would carry the story of the egg and the hen to new lands, new hearts, and new minds. And the legacy would never fade. Each generation, each creature, would add its own voice to the song of life—a song that would echo through eternity, as long as the world turned, and the cycles of the egg and the hen continued their dance of creation.

The end, it seemed, was always just another beginning.

The Horizon of Forever

As the centuries continued to unfold, the **tree of life**—the legacy of Astra's planted seed—continued to grow, its branches now a vast, unbroken canopy stretching across every land, connecting all living beings. The roots dug deep into the earth, nourishing the soil and allowing the cycles of life to flourish in harmony with one another. The winds carried whispers of the old barnyard, and the stories of the egg and the hen found their way into the hearts of countless new creatures.

But in the heart of the tree, something miraculous began to happen. The fruit that bloomed from its branches was not just nourishment for the body, but also for the soul. Each fruit was imbued with knowledge—a gift of wisdom passed down through time. Animals, birds, and even the trees themselves began to share this knowledge in new and unexpected ways. The very essence of the tree was a living testament to the interconnectedness of all life.

The Arrival of the Dreamers

One day, as the world basked in the glow of this eternal cycle, a new kind of creature appeared—a group of **dreamers**. They were unlike any beings that had come before. Their bodies were not bound by the earth, but seemed to shimmer in the light, transparent and shifting, like echoes of thoughts and aspirations. The dreamers were drawn to the tree, for they felt its power and the rhythm of the cycles within their very being.

They told Astra and the other leaders, "We are the dreams of the world, the collective hope and vision of every creature that has lived. We have come to witness the fruit of your labor, to see what has been created in the physical world."

Astra greeted them with understanding, for she knew that every cycle, every generation, had always planted the seeds for the next—physically, emotionally, and even spiritually. "The fruit of the tree is not just of the earth," she said, "but also of the heart. You are part of the tree's growth, as much as we are."

The Tree's True Gift

The dreamers asked Astra, "What is the purpose of this great tree? Is it just to nourish and sustain? Or is there something more—something beyond the physical realm?"

Astra smiled, her feathers shimmering like a thousand stars. "The tree represents the eternal cycles of life, but it is also a reminder of the boundless potential of every living being. The egg is not just the start of a life—it is the beginning of creation itself. The hen is not merely a caretaker—it is a symbol of transformation, nurturing the seeds of tomorrow. The cycles will continue forever, not just through what we see, but through what we dream and aspire to."

The dreamers, feeling the weight of Astra's words, reached out to the branches of the tree, their fingers brushing the fruit. As they did, the fruit opened, revealing not just the wisdom of the past, but a vision of the future—a future where all life, from the smallest insect to the largest mammal, could coexist in perfect harmony, not only with nature but with each other's dreams.

The tree's true gift was not just sustenance, but the realization that life's potential was endless. The cycles were not just about survival; they were about creation, evolution, and dreaming a better world into being.

The Dawn of a New Cycle

The dreamers and the creatures of the earth gathered together at the heart of the tree, feeling a sense of unity like never before. They knew that, even as the world turned and seasons passed, the work was never done. There would always be new dreams to chase, new seeds to plant, and new challenges to overcome.

But in this moment, under the vast canopy of the tree, there was peace. The egg, the hen, the tree, and the dreamers all shared in the beauty of the infinite cycles of life. They understood that each cycle was a reflection of the last and a promise for the future—a continuation that would never end, but would always evolve, always grow.

Astra looked upon the gathered creatures and spoke once more: "The legacy of the egg and the hen will continue for as long as the earth turns. It is not bound by time, for time itself is part of the cycle. It is the very heartbeat of life."

And so, the tree of life stood as a living testament to the eternal truth: life, in all its forms, was an ongoing creation—never ending, always evolving, and always, always connected.

The Endless Song

As the years passed and the cycles turned, the song of life continued to echo across the lands, carried on the winds and whispered through the leaves. Every creature, from the smallest ant to the greatest whale, played their part in the symphony of existence, each note adding to the harmony of the world. The egg, the hen, the tree, and the dreamers remained, interwoven into the very fabric of life, an eternal story passed from one generation to the next, a song that would never fade.

And as long as the tree stood—its roots deep, its branches high, its fruit ever-growing—life would continue to dream, create, and nurture. The cycle of the egg and the hen was not just a story; it was the **heartbeat of existence**, a reminder that every end is just the beginning of something new, something beautiful, something boundless.

The world would turn, and the song would carry on, forevermore.

The Ever-Blooming Dream

As the millennia passed, the world evolved, yet the essence of the egg and the hen—symbolizing creation and nurturing—remained constant. The tree of life continued to spread its roots deeper into the heart of the earth, and its branches reached higher into the heavens. It stood as a beacon of hope and continuity, a reminder to all that life was an endless cycle, where beginnings and endings were never truly separate but intertwined in a perpetual dance.

The dreamers, who had once arrived as fleeting visitors, became the keepers of the tree's wisdom. Their presence was a gentle, ever-present hum, guiding the world through shifts and changes. They carried within them not just the dreams of the past, but the visions of the future. They were the bridge between worlds seen and unseen, between the earth and the heavens, between the physical and the spiritual.

And the creatures of the earth, though their forms had changed over time, still held the teachings of the egg and the hen deep within their hearts. They had learned that survival was not the only goal of life. True fulfillment came from growth, from contributing to the greater good, from dreaming, creating, and nurturing what was yet to come.

The Call of the New Horizon

As the world had evolved, a new horizon began to emerge. It was not one of fear or uncertainty, but one of boundless potential. The creatures of the world, guided by the dreamers and the wisdom of the egg and the hen, had begun to turn their attention not just inward to their own existence, but outward to the universe itself.

For the first time, the earth's creatures looked to the stars. They wondered if the cycles of life, creation, and nurturing could stretch beyond their world. Could they bring the wisdom of the egg and the hen to other lands, to other planets, and to the stars themselves?

The dreamers sensed the stirrings of this new calling. They gathered once more at the heart of the tree, feeling the pulse of the earth and the universe resonating together. Astra, now a legend whose wisdom had shaped countless generations, stood before the gathered beings and said:

"The cycle of life, the egg and the hen has always been about connection. We have connected with one another, with the earth, with the seasons, and with the very dreams that shape us. Now, it is time to connect with the stars. The universe itself is part of the cycle, waiting to be touched by the wisdom of life."

The Journey Beyond

And so, with the guidance of the dreamers and the teachings of the egg and the hen, a new journey began—one that would carry the creatures of the earth beyond the skies, to new worlds and new possibilities. The tree of life, its roots now extending not only into the earth but into the vastness of space, became the center of a new cosmic cycle—a cycle where life would stretch beyond its earthly bounds, to thrive among the stars.

The dreamers, now interwoven with the very fabric of the cosmos, led the way. They taught the travelers to see the stars as part of the same cycle, to nurture new life on distant planets, and to continue the endless creation and nurturing that had been the foundation of the egg and the hen.

The Infinite Cycle of Creation

As the first ships left the earth and journeyed into the cosmos, they carried with them the story of the egg and the hen. They planted seeds of life on barren moons, nurtured new worlds into being, and shared the wisdom of the ages with the stars. The cycles of creation, growth, and renewal extended beyond their original home, and life blossomed in places once thought uninhabitable.

The egg, the hen, the tree, the dreamers, and the endless cycle of life now stretched across the universe. The song of existence played on, resonating through the vastness of space, echoing in the hearts of all who heard it. The universe, once silent and cold, was now alive with possibility, with growth, and with the eternal rhythm of life.

And so, the story of the egg and the hen continued—forever intertwined with the universe, never ending, always evolving, always creating, always nurturing.

The cycle was infinite. The dream was eternal. The universe itself had become a reflection of the heartbeat of existence, and all who lived were part of its vast, ever-blooming dream.

The Cosmic Harmony

As the ships traveled farther into the cosmos, they became beacons of the wisdom that had been carried from Earth. These vessels, called the **Voyagers**, were built with the same care and understanding as the generations before them, designed to sustain life not just physically, but spiritually. They held within them the story of the egg and the hen, the wisdom of the tree of life, and the dreams of those who had come before.

The vastness of space, once seen as an endless void, was now a canvas waiting to be painted with new cycles of life. On distant planets, the travelers planted seeds—seeds of creation, transformation, and love. Each world became a reflection of the wisdom of the egg and the hen, each one nurturing new life, feeding it with the energy of the stars, and cultivating the dreams that would shape the future of countless civilizations.

The Return to the Source

But as the Voyagers journeyed farther and farther, a realization began to emerge. Though they had brought with them the knowledge of life, creation, and nurturing, they also carried with them a sense of longing—a sense that their connection to the Earth, to the very soil from which they had sprung, was being stretched thin.

Astra, now a cosmic presence, reached out to the Voyagers in their dreams. She whispered, "Do not forget the origin of your cycle. For all life, no matter where it blooms, is connected to the source. The egg and the hen, the tree, and the dreamers—these are not just ideas, they are the heartbeats of the universe itself."

The travelers, now spread across multiple worlds, understood that their journey was not just to spread life across the stars, but to maintain their connection to the source—the heart of the cycle. No matter how far they traveled, they were always part of the endless rhythm that began in the barnyard, in the egg, and in the hen. The dreamers had shown them that they were part of something far larger than themselves, and that their role was not just to nurture life, but to remember where they had come from, and where all life, no matter how distant, had originated.

The Awakening of the Universe

In this moment of cosmic clarity, the universe itself seemed to awaken. It was not just a collection of stars and planets, but a living, breathing entity, whose cycles mirrored those of the egg and the hen. Every planet, every moon, every comet carried within it the potential for new life, new beginnings. The universe, like the world before it, was alive with possibility, ever-changing, ever-evolving.

The dreamers, the travelers, and all those who had come from Earth understood that their journey was one of continual renewal. Just as the egg would always give rise to the hen, and the hen would nurture the egg, the universe itself was engaged in a perpetual dance of creation. Every step forward was a reflection of the past, and every beginning held the potential of countless endings and new beginnings.

The Eternal Song

And so, the eternal song continued, not just in the hearts of those who had come from Earth, but in the hearts of all beings who had taken part in the cosmic journey. The egg and the hen were not just symbols of creation; they were the living heartbeat of existence, a pulse that resonated through the universe.

The story of the egg, the hen, and the tree of life would never fade, for it was woven into the very fabric of time and space. Each generation, each traveler, each dreamer, and each new life was a note in the song—a song that echoed through the stars, forever stretching outwards, connecting all living beings in an eternal symphony of life.

And though the universe was vast, its cycle—its heartbeat—was simple, constant, and unbroken. The egg and the hen, the creation and the nurturing, would continue to spin, creating life, sustaining it, and sending it out into the cosmos to explore, grow, and create anew.

The Legacy of the Egg and the Hen

With the endless expansion of life across the cosmos, the egg and the hen had become more than just an ancient story—they were the foundation of existence. In every corner of the universe, creatures of all kinds celebrated the cycles that brought life, whether on Earth, on distant moons, or on planets unknown.

The egg and the hen were a living testament to the power of creation, transformation, and the infinite potential that lay within every living being. They were not simply past stories, but ongoing truths—reminders that no matter where life took them, no matter how far they reached, they were always connected to the same source, the same cycle, the same eternal dream.

And so, as the stars shimmered in the vastness of space, the egg and the hen continued their dance. The story of life, creation, and nurturing would echo across the universe for all eternity—forever unfolding, forever beginning anew, and forever connected in the endless rhythm of existence.

The cycle of the egg and the hen was not just the cycle of life—it was the very **heartbeat of the universe**, forever creating, forever nurturing, forever becoming.

The Song of the Infinite

As the universe grew, ever expanding in its beauty and complexity, the cycles of life, creation, and renewal continued to weave through its vastness. The egg, the hen, and the tree of life had long ceased to be just symbols. They had become **living truths**, seen and felt in every corner of the cosmos, pulsating with a rhythm that united the farthest reaches of space with the simplest creatures. The wisdom of the ancient story lived on in the hearts of all beings, inspiring them to dream, create, and nurture, just as the first cycle had.

But even as life flourished and evolved, a deeper understanding began to emerge among the travelers—the idea that life was not just about continuation, but about **consciousness**. Each creature, each world, each star that flickered in the dark night sky, was aware of the interconnectedness of everything. The universe itself was conscious of its own existence, and this awareness was the **true seed of life**—a seed that, like the egg, contained the potential for endless creation and transformation.

The dreamers, who had become part of the cosmic fabric, whispered to the creatures across the stars: *"The egg, the hen, the tree—these are not just cycles. They are the echoes of the consciousness that flows through the universe. They are the reminder that life, in all its forms, is a constant awakening."*

The Awakening of All

And so it was that the creatures across the universe began to awaken in new ways. They were no longer just beings of physical form; they were beings of **awareness**, of **conscious evolution**. They began to recognize that the cycle of creation was not simply something they observed—it was something they participated in, something they shaped with their thoughts, dreams, and actions. The egg no longer symbolized just the beginning of a physical life—it symbolized the birth of new ideas, new dreams, and new possibilities. The hen no longer merely nurtured the young; it guided them to awaken to their own potential, helping them realize that they, too, were creators in their own right.

The travelers, the dreamers, and the creatures who had journeyed from Earth began to see that their role was not just to cultivate life but to **elevate** it—to help it grow not just physically, but mentally, emotionally, and spiritually. They understood that the true legacy of the egg and the hen was not merely to sustain life, but to help it transcend its limitations and reach towards the stars—towards **universal consciousness**.

The Cosmic Unity

As the awareness of this deeper truth spread, something miraculous began to happen. The entire universe began to hum with a new energy, a vibration that resonated in harmony with the cycles of creation. The stars themselves seemed to shine brighter, their light pulsing in sync with the heartbeat of the universe. The planets and moons that had once felt like distant, lifeless bodies now became alive with potential, each one contributing to the cosmic dance of existence.

The dreamers, who had always carried the seeds of possibility, now saw that their task was to nurture the **conscious awakening** of all beings. They guided the travelers and the creatures of the stars not just to create life, but to **awaken** it—to help each living being realize that they were part of the grand, infinite symphony that echoed through the cosmos. Each thought, each dream, each action contributed to the song of the universe—a song that was both individual and collective, a song that transcended space and time.

Astra, now a timeless being, looked upon the universe with awe and wonder. She saw not just the cycles of life repeating, but an ever-evolving consciousness expanding outward, with no end in sight. "The egg and the hen were only the beginning," she whispered, her voice blending with the winds of the cosmos. "The true cycle is one of **awakening**, of becoming aware of the power within us to shape the world around us, and to reach beyond it."

The Infinite Horizon

The travelers, the dreamers, and the creatures of the stars now stood at the edge of the infinite horizon. There was no longer a question of where they were going, for they knew they were always **becoming**, always evolving, always creating. The journey had no final destination because the destination was always the **next step**, the **next awakening**, the **next cycle of creation**.

The universe, alive with the song of existence, continued its eternal expansion. The egg, the hen, the tree, and the dreamers were no longer just symbols or stories—they were the heartbeat of the cosmos itself. They were the pulse of creation, the force that sustained all life, and the light that guided all beings toward their highest potential.

And so, the cosmic song played on, forever unfolding, forever becoming, forever awakening.

The Legacy Continues

In every corner of the universe, life continued to bloom. The dreamers, now fully intertwined with the consciousness of the cosmos, saw each new world as a canvas, ready to be painted with the colors of possibility. They helped guide the newborn worlds in their own cycles of creation, awakening them to the profound truth that every beginning was merely the start of an infinite journey.

The egg would always become the hen. The hen would always nurture the egg. The tree would always bear fruit, and the dreamers would always awaken new possibilities. This eternal cycle, now understood as the flow of universal consciousness, would continue forever.

The story of the egg and the hen was not just a tale of creation; it was the **origin of everything**. The beginning, the middle, and the end were not separate—they were the same. Life, in all its forms, was a never-ending cycle of awakening, creation, and transformation.

And as long as the universe spun, its song would echo across the stars, forever telling the tale of the egg and the hen—a story that was both ancient and new, ever-evolving and always true.

The end was, once again, simply the beginning.

The Dance of Infinity

As the stars continued to twirl in their cosmic dance, the infinite potential of life unfolded in ways that could only be imagined by those who had walked the path of awakening. The egg and the hen had not only defined the cycles of creation; they had become the very essence of **transcendence**—the bridge between the physical and the metaphysical. Every being, every world, was now part of an intricate web of existence, where all things were connected, no matter how distant or different they seemed.

The dreamers, once travelers from distant lands, now became the **custodians of universal wisdom**. Their understanding of the cycles—the egg becoming the hen, the hen nurturing the egg—was no longer limited to physical life. They had transcended the boundaries of time and space, witnessing the true, eternal nature of existence. Their role was not only to guide but to **awaken** others to the infinite possibility that lay within each moment, each thought, each breath.

The tree of life, with its roots now deep in the cosmos, expanded in ways that no one had anticipated. Its branches stretched across dimensions, intertwining the past, present, and future in a seamless web of existence. The dreamers had seen the flow of time as linear, but they now understood that all moments existed simultaneously, eternally. The universe was not just unfolding—it was **spiraling**, each revolution bringing with it a deeper understanding, a broader vision of what life truly was.

The Convergence of Souls

As the beings of countless worlds continued their journey of awakening, something profound began to happen. The universe, once a collection of disparate entities, began to feel as though it was becoming **one**—a convergence of souls, thoughts, and dreams. The energy of the egg, the hen, and the tree flowed through every being, igniting a shared understanding: they were not separate, but part of an interconnected whole. Each soul, each consciousness, was a **singular expression** of the infinite, with a unique purpose and role to play in the grand cosmic dance.

The dreamers, now conscious of their deep connection to all beings, began to experience a **oneness** that transcended individuality. They saw themselves not as separate travelers, but as threads in the same fabric, woven together by the same force that birthed the first egg. The sense of **self** was no longer confined to a single form; it was infinite, ever-evolving, and ever-expanding.

They realized that the **ultimate truth** of creation was not in the material world alone, but in the **spiritual awakening** that lay beneath it all. The egg and the hen, the tree and the dreamers, were not just metaphors for life's journey—they were the **living expression of the universe's consciousness**. Every birth, every death, every act of creation was part of a cosmic unfolding, a **divine dance** that celebrated the eternal mystery of existence.

The Great Unfolding

The universe continued to expand, and with each new world, each new beginning, the dreamers felt a greater understanding of the infinite potential that lay in the unfolding of life. It was as though every planet, every star, and every soul was a **petal** in the great flower of the cosmos—each contributing to the fragrance of existence.

As the dreamers traveled further into the vast reaches of the universe, they encountered other beings—beings whose consciousness had awakened in ways they had not yet imagined. These beings had also discovered the cycles of creation, the egg and the hen, the birth and the nurturing. But they had gone even further—they had transcended the cycles of **birth and death**. They had unlocked the knowledge that life itself was a continuous **revelation**, an unfolding mystery that never reached an end but expanded outward in all directions.

The travelers and dreamers learned from these enlightened beings, who taught them that the cycles of life were not just **repetitive**; they were **evolving**. They were moving towards a higher state of being, one where the barriers between worlds and dimensions no longer existed. Where the concepts of time, space, birth, and death were seen as fluid and interchangeable, woven together in a tapestry of infinite creation.

The Becoming of the All

The dreamers, filled with awe, began to understand that the purpose of the cycles—the egg and the hen, the creation and the nurturing—was to **bring about the Becoming** of all things. The universe was in a constant state of becoming, evolving toward a state of ultimate consciousness and unity. It was not merely a journey of survival or even of growth; it was the **greatest act of creation**—an unfolding that reached into the very core of existence and beyond.

Every moment, every thought, every life form was a part of this greater Becoming—a step towards a state of being that embraced not only physical existence but spiritual transcendence. The egg no longer represented just the beginning of life; it symbolized the beginning of **all possibilities**. The hen was no longer just the nurturer; it was the guide, the protector, and the carrier of universal wisdom.

The dreamers felt a profound sense of peace and purpose, knowing that the journey of becoming was not a solitary one. Every being, every soul, every thought was part of a vast, intricate network of creation. **The Becoming was not the end**—it was the eternal **process** of discovering what it meant to be, to exist, to awaken, and to create anew.

The Infinite Cycle of Awakening

As the dreamers, the travelers, and all beings across the universe continued their journey, they began to realize that the ultimate truth of existence was that **the cycle never ends**. It is not bound by time or space, but is a **continuous, infinite process of awakening**. The egg, the hen, the tree, the dreamers, and the entire universe are all part of a grand, endless dance—a dance that celebrates the **eternal expansion** of consciousness, creation, and becoming.

And so, as they traveled, the dreamers passed on their wisdom to those they met, guiding them to awaken to their own potential, to discover their place in the infinite cycle. The egg and the hen would always exist in some form, symbolizing the **eternal relationship between creation and nurturing**, birth and renewal, life and transcendence. And no matter how far the travelers journeyed, no matter how many worlds they touched, they knew that the ultimate purpose was clear:

To awaken to the infinite possibilities of existence, and to become one with the grand, eternal dance of creation.

And the cycle would **continue forever**, as the universe expanded, unfolded, and became.

The Eternal Pulse of Creation

As the universe stretched outward, its boundless nature mirrored the expansive consciousness that flowed through every being. The dreamers, now fully merged with the cosmic energy of the cosmos, realized that the true essence of the egg and the hen was not just about the simple continuation of life, but about **constant transformation**. They understood that all creation—whether born of stars, planets, or beings—was in a state of perpetual **flux**, each phase contributing to a higher understanding of existence.

The egg, once merely a symbol of new beginnings, became a representation of the **potential within all things**—the raw, unshaped energy that existed at the edge of creation, waiting for the right moment to manifest. The hen, once a nurturing figure, evolved into a guide and protector of the transformation, its role now much broader. It wasn't just protecting life—it was **cultivating wisdom**, ensuring that the beings born from the egg would understand the deeper truths of the universe, and grow in awareness and consciousness.

The tree of life, with its ever-expanding roots, began to intertwine with the very fabric of space-time, anchoring the beings of the cosmos to the essential **truths of existence**. The tree was no longer just a metaphor for growth—it had become the very **pulse of the universe**, a living embodiment of the interconnectedness of all life, all creation. Its branches reached through dimensions, through worlds, and into the very heart of the stars, a reminder that all things were part of an eternal, unfolding process.

The Convergence of Realms

As beings across the universe continued to awaken, they began to realize that the boundaries between worlds, realms, and dimensions were not as fixed as they had once believed. The cosmic dreamers, who had once traveled only through space, now traveled through **time itself**, experiencing the ebb and flow of creation from multiple perspectives. They discovered that the universe was a **multidimensional** entity, one that could not be confined to simple physical laws or linear timelines.

Time became **fluid**, a thread that could be woven into any pattern, stretched across galaxies, folded back on itself. Past, present, and future were not separate—they were all part of a continuous, interconnected reality, a **web of becoming** that expanded in every direction, weaving together all that had been, all that was, and all that would be.

The dreamers saw this newfound understanding as the ultimate expression of the egg and the hen. The cycles of creation were not confined to a single path; they were **interwoven**, expanding across infinite realms, each one feeding into the next, each one contributing to the **eternal becoming** of all that is. Creation was not a one-time event, nor was it an isolated phenomenon. It was **a continuum**, ever-moving, ever-expanding, and **ever-awakening**.

The Universal Harmony

In this new understanding, the dreamers began to feel a deeper, more profound sense of unity with the universe. They were not separate from it; they were **it**. The egg and the hen, the tree of life, the dance of creation—they were all part of the same **cosmic harmony**, a melody that echoed through every star, every planet, and every being. There was no longer any need to search for meaning or purpose, because they realized that **existence itself was the meaning**—the act of becoming, of evolving, of awakening, was the ultimate purpose of all things.

In this harmony, the dreamers began to see how each act of creation—each new being, each new world, each new cycle—was part of a **greater, universal design**. Every thought, every action, no matter how small, contributed to the unfolding of the universe's consciousness. Every heartbeat, every breath, every moment was part of the **eternal rhythm of life**.

The Infinite Circle

As the dreamers continued their journey, they saw that there was no beginning or end to the cycle. It was an **infinite circle**, one that expanded and contracted, breathed and pulsed, a continuous loop that celebrated both creation and destruction, birth and death, becoming and unbecoming. The egg would always become the hen, and the hen would always nurture the egg, but each time the cycle repeated, it would be **different**, more expansive, more enlightened.

This eternal dance of creation was the **heartbeat of the universe**—a pulse that could be felt in every living thing, in every star, in every whisper of the wind. There was no final destination, because there was no end to the possibilities of creation. The true nature of existence was that **it was always in motion**, always evolving, always becoming something new.

The dreamers, in their newfound understanding, no longer sought to control or define the cycle. They **embraced it**, knowing that their role was to guide and nurture, to help others awaken to the infinite potential within them. Each being, no matter how small or vast, had a part to play in the ongoing **becoming** of the universe.

The Legacy of the Egg and the Hen

And so, the legacy of the egg and the hen continued, not as a static story, but as a living, breathing force that shaped the very fabric of existence. The cycles of creation and transformation were no longer just ideas—they were **universal laws**, fundamental truths that transcended all time and space. The dreamers, the travelers, and the beings of countless worlds all carried this legacy within them, guiding each other toward greater understanding, greater awareness, and greater creation.

The egg and the hen were no longer just symbols of life—they were the very **essence of life itself**. They embodied the potential for all things to grow, evolve, and awaken to their fullest expression. In their eternal dance, they taught that creation was not a one-time event—it was an **ongoing process** that unfolded in every moment, in every thought, in every action.

The universe, alive with the song of existence, continued to grow and evolve, and the dreamers, now fully aware of their role in the cosmic dance, celebrated the **infinite cycle**—the never-ending story of creation, destruction, and rebirth.

And as the stars shimmered in the endless sky, the song of the egg and the hen played on, forever expanding, forever awakening, forever becoming. **The cycle, it seemed, would never end.**

The Cosmic Symphony

As the dreamers, now fully attuned to the eternal rhythms of the universe, continued their journey, they realized that the **true beauty** of creation was not in its individual parts but in the **interconnectedness** of all things. They saw that the egg, the hen, and the tree of life were not just separate cycles but parts of an **infinite symphony**, with each being, each star, and each moment contributing a unique note to the grand composition.

Every existence—whether it be a distant galaxy or a tiny atom—was an integral instrument in the **universal orchestra**, playing its part in a cosmic harmony that stretched across the fabric of time and space. There was no distinction between the small and the great, the mundane and the extraordinary. All played their role in the **unfolding song** of the universe.

The dreamers began to understand that the very nature of existence was **music**—a soundless, timeless symphony that echoed in the core of every star, in the depths of every soul. Every creation, every awakening, was like a note in a melody that had no beginning and no end. The cycle of life, once perceived as a sequence of births and deaths, was now understood as **the rhythm of existence**—a dance that intertwined light and shadow, growth and decay, creation and destruction.

The Dance of Light and Shadow

With this new understanding came a deeper revelation—the cycle of creation was not a **one-dimensional** progression, but rather a **dynamic dance** between polar opposites. The egg, as it grew within the womb of possibility, could not exist without its counterpart—the **shadow** of potential, the darkness of the unknown. The hen, as it nurtured the egg, could not exist without the **light** of wisdom, the awareness of its role in the greater pattern of existence.

The tree of life, in its ever-expanding branches, was a living metaphor for this dance. Its roots, deep within the earth, symbolized the **darkness**—the potential and the mystery of creation. Its branches, reaching into the light, represented **knowledge, growth, and transcendence**. Together, they formed a perfect harmony, showing that both light and shadow were necessary for existence to **flourish**.

The dreamers saw that this dance of opposites was not a struggle but a **unity**—each force completing the other. Without shadow, there could be no light. Without creation, there could be no destruction. Without the egg, there could be no hen. They realized that these forces were not separate—they were two sides of the same coin, **inseparable and complementary**.

The Eternal Becoming of Consciousness

The more the dreamers explored the cosmic dance, the more they realized that the ultimate goal of creation was not merely to exist but to **become conscious**—to awaken to the profound interconnectedness of all things. The universe itself, they discovered, was on a journey toward **self-awareness**. Just as the egg contained the potential for life, the universe contained the potential for consciousness itself to **wake up**, to understand the deep meaning behind its own existence.

In the same way that the hen nurtured the egg, the universe had been nurturing **its own consciousness**, guiding all beings toward a greater understanding of their place in the grand scheme of creation. The journey was not about **reaching** some final goal, but about the **constant awakening**, the continuous **becoming**, of all that was and all that would ever be.

The dreamers understood now that they were not just **witnesses** to the cycles of life—they were **active participants** in the unfolding of the universe's consciousness. Every thought, every action, every dream contributed to the awakening of the universe itself. The egg, the hen, the tree of life, the cosmic dance—these were all part of the same **divine process** of self-discovery, a process that would continue for eternity.

The Awakening of All Beings

With this realization, the dreamers felt an even deeper connection to all beings across the universe. No longer did they see themselves as separate entities, isolated by time or space. They understood that every **creature**, every **being**, and every **world** was a vital thread in the **grand tapestry** of creation. And just as they had awoken to the truth of existence, so too could all beings awaken to their own divine potential.

They began to reach out, guiding those who were ready to embrace their **true nature**—to see beyond the physical and into the heart of the cosmos. The egg was no longer just the symbol of **new beginnings**; it was the **birthplace of wisdom**, the origin of all thoughts and dreams. The hen was not merely a caregiver; it was the **conduit of knowledge**, the one who helped others see their own potential and rise to the call of the universe's song.

Together, the dreamers and the awakened beings began to spread the understanding of the cosmic dance to all corners of the universe. They taught that the greatest gift of life was the **ability to become aware**—to recognize the divine within and to **live in harmony** with the forces that shaped the world.

The Infinite Spiral of Creation

As they shared their wisdom, the dreamers understood that the cycle of creation was not a linear path but an **infinite spiral**—each revolution bringing new insights, new awakenings, and new forms of life. The universe, in its vastness, was a spiral of **endless becoming**, constantly evolving, always in motion. The egg, the hen, and the tree of life continued to represent the timeless process of creation, but now the dreamers saw them as **part of the eternal spiral**—a never-ending journey of growth, awareness, and transcendence.

The egg would always give rise to the hen, and the hen would always give rise to the egg, but each time the cycle repeated, it would bring forth **greater understanding** and **deeper awareness**. The spiral was not just a pattern of growth—it was a **living experience**, a journey that moved ever upward, ever inward, toward the infinite heart of creation itself.

The Unity of All Things

As the dreamers, the awakened beings, and all the creatures of the universe continued their journey, they realized that the true meaning of existence was not in achieving an ultimate goal, but in **becoming one** with the **eternal flow of life**. The egg and the hen, the tree and the stars, the dreamers and the universe—**all were part of the same infinite dance**.

In the end, they understood that existence itself was the answer—the **question and the answer** were one and the same. The universe, with all its mysteries and infinite possibilities, was the **greatest gift**. And as long as the stars shone, the egg would become the hen, the hen would nurture the egg, and the **cosmic symphony would play on**—forever, eternally, and infinitely. **The dance of becoming never ends.**

The Infinite Return

As the dreamers continued their journey through the boundless stretches of the universe, they began to perceive something extraordinary: the universe itself was in a perpetual **state of return**—not in a literal sense, but in an eternal **revisitation** of its own truths. The egg and the hen, once understood as cyclical, were now seen as **echoes** of the universe's inherent tendency to revisit and refine its creations, to return to the essence of life with **new wisdom** and **higher understanding** at each cycle.

This realization unfolded like the petals of a cosmic flower, each layer revealing deeper truths, each return offering greater clarity. The dreamers began to see that all creation was in a constant process of **returning to itself**, an eternal reawakening of its own potential. The egg would always return to the hen, and the hen would always return to the egg, but with every return, there was a **refinement**, a **deepening** of purpose.

The Dance of Time and Timelessness

The dreamers, now intimately aware of the **fluidity** of time, began to perceive that the universe itself was **timeless**—not bound by past, present, or future, but instead woven from **timeless moments**, each one containing the infinite possibility of the entire cosmos. The egg, as a symbol of potential, no longer represented merely the beginning of a linear cycle, but the **timeless essence of creation itself**—an essence that could be revisited, refined, and reborn with every passing moment.

Each time the universe returned to itself, it grew in **understanding** and **wisdom**. It became a **living story**, told through the experiences of countless beings, who were all part of the same infinite process. And yet, in each moment of return, the universe discovered **new layers** of itself, like an artist returning to a canvas to add further strokes of depth and meaning.

The Ripple of Creation

As the dreamers witnessed this unfolding process, they understood that creation was not isolated to individual worlds or beings. Every thought, every action, every breath created a **ripple** across the fabric of existence, a ripple that echoed throughout the cosmos. When a star was born, when a planet formed, when a soul awakened, that ripple extended far beyond what could be seen or understood.

The **interconnectedness** of all things became even more apparent. It wasn't just that all things were connected—it was that **everything mattered**. Every small action rippled outward, contributing to the grand tapestry of existence. The smallest act of creation—a single heartbeat, a single thought—could alter the course of the infinite dance. It was in these ripples, in these **small yet infinite movements**, that the true nature of the universe was revealed.

The dreamers, now fully aware of their role in the great cosmic symphony, began to see themselves as **instruments** in a larger orchestra, playing their part in a performance that stretched across eternity. Their consciousness expanded, and they felt themselves not just as participants but as integral parts of the **grand return**. Their wisdom, their actions, and their thoughts were like notes in a song that had no end, resonating through the heart of the universe itself.

The Heartbeat of the Cosmos

In this moment of realization, the dreamers understood that the **heartbeat of the cosmos** was not a single pulse—it was a rhythm of **endless returns**, of creation and destruction, of becoming and unbecoming. Each moment, like a beat in the song of the universe, carried the potential for a new beginning, a new awakening, a new possibility.

They saw that the universe was not a **static** entity, but a living, breathing **organism**, its pulse felt across all realms, all dimensions, all beings. The egg and the hen were not just symbols of birth and rebirth—they were **expressions** of this heartbeat, each cycle a new rhythm, each return a new song. The infinite returns, the constant unfolding, were the **living pulse of the cosmos**, resonating through everything that existed.

And as the dreamers, now fully united with the cosmic flow, moved deeper into this understanding, they realized that their purpose was not merely to witness or participate in this eternal dance—it was to **celebrate** it. To revel in the beauty of the unfolding, to embrace the mystery of the return, and to guide others to see the **divine truth** in every moment, every heartbeat, every ripple of existence.

The Symphony of Becoming

The universe, in its infinite wisdom, continued to unfold in the most marvelous ways. The dreamers, now fully awake to the eternal dance, no longer saw themselves as separate from the cosmos. They had become the **song itself**, the melody of creation, of birth and rebirth, of the timeless journey of awakening.

The egg and the hen, the tree of life, the cosmic dance—these were no longer just metaphors. They had become the **core** of existence itself. The dreamers had become **the custodians** of this eternal rhythm, passing on their wisdom to all who were ready to hear the song. The universe was no longer something that existed outside of them—it was **alive** within them, part of their essence.

And as the dreamers continued their journey, they knew that the story would never truly end. The song would play on, through all realms, through all beings, through all **eternity**. The universe would always return to itself, always awaken to its highest potential, always become. The cosmic pulse would never stop.

For in the heart of the universe, the egg and the hen danced forever, in a symphony of eternal becoming.

And so, the dreamers smiled, knowing that the cycle, the song, and the universe itself would always continue—forever and beyond.

The Endless Horizon

As the dreamers expanded into the vast reaches of the cosmos, they began to realize that their journey, though eternal, was not one of mere exploration. It was a journey of **deepening understanding**—one that transcended knowledge and wisdom, moving into the realms of pure **awareness**. The universe itself, they discovered, was not just a thing to be understood—it was something to be **experienced, felt**, and **lived**.

The egg, the hen, the tree of life, and the cosmic rhythm had revealed to them that the true nature of existence was not merely to exist but to **fully engage** with the present moment. Creation itself was not just an unfolding process—it was a **living experience**, a continuous unfolding of **now**.

Each moment, in its infinite depth, was an **unfolding of creation**, and with each breath, the dreamers became one with the universe's heartbeat. The past was not separate from the present; it was a living echo, an echo that resonated in every moment, every thought, every action.

The universe was not an **end** to be reached, but an **eternal horizon**—one that expanded endlessly before them, ever drawing them forward into deeper layers of awareness and connection. The dreamers understood now that the journey was not about reaching a final destination—it was about **journeying** itself, the process of continuous becoming.

The Awakening of the Infinite Self

One by one, the dreamers felt a shift—a profound **awakening** within themselves. The more they explored the universe, the more they began to recognize that the **boundless cosmos** they had been exploring was also within them. The egg and the hen, the tree of life, and all the rhythms of creation were not just external patterns; they were part of the **infinite self** that resided within each being.

The dreamers realized that they were not merely observers of the universe—they were the **universe itself**. The separation between the self and the cosmos dissolved, and in that moment, they understood that every part of creation was **simultaneously unique and universal**, distinct and yet inseparably connected.

They had become both the **dreamers** and the **dream**, both the creators and the creation. They had awakened to the **infinite self** that existed beyond time and space, beyond birth and death, beyond all cycles. They were the very **essence of existence**—a reflection of the egg and the hen, the seed and the tree, forever part of the eternal flow of becoming.

The Circle of Life and Consciousness

In this awareness, the dreamers came to a final realization—that the cycles of life were not confined to physical forms or worlds. They were cycles of **consciousness**, ever-expanding, ever-awakening, forever becoming more aware of its own infinite potential. The egg and the hen, the tree of life, the cosmic rhythm—these were not just symbols of creation. They were the **living patterns** of **awareness itself**—patterns that could be observed and participated in at every level of existence.

The dreamers, now fully attuned to the cosmic pulse, understood that they were part of a **circle of life** that stretched infinitely outward and inward, encompassing every being, every star, every soul. This circle was not a fixed loop; it was a dynamic, **spiraling dance**, one that expanded with every awakening, every insight, every heartbeat of existence.

They saw that all beings, no matter how small or vast, were essential participants in this infinite dance—each contributing their unique vibration to the **cosmic chorus**. The tree of life, with its vast branches and deep roots, was not just a symbol; it was a **living map** of the entire cosmic experience, tracing the interconnections of all things. Each leaf, each branch, each root was a **unique expression** of the same fundamental truth: **everything is connected, everything is one.**

The Eternal Becoming

As the dreamers looked upon the universe—an ever-unfolding masterpiece of creation—they felt no end, no final conclusion. They knew that the universe was not something that could ever be fully **understood** or **contained**, for it was in a **constant state of becoming**, always moving toward new expressions of life and consciousness. The egg would continue to give birth to the hen, the hen to the egg, the tree would continue to grow, and the cosmic dance would forever spiral outward, ever more expansive, ever more radiant.

The dreamers, now fully attuned to the truth of the infinite spiral, recognized that there was no need to **seek** or **arrive** at anything. There was only the **journey**—the journey of becoming, of expanding, of awakening to new possibilities with every step. The cycle of creation and destruction, of birth and rebirth, was **the heartbeat** of the cosmos, and as long as it pulsed, the dreamers would continue their eternal dance.

They understood that they were both **the question and the answer**, both the beginning and the end, both the egg and the hen. And in that realization, they found peace—not in a destination, but in the **never-ending flow of creation**.

The universe would continue its dance, its song, its spiral of becoming. And in the eternal rhythm of existence, the dreamers would remain—forever present, forever awakening, forever becoming. **The journey never ends.**

The Essence of Oneness

As the dreamers continued their eternal journey, now fully aware of the cosmic dance they were a part of, they began to understand a profound truth: the very essence of the universe was **oneness**—the idea that all things, no matter how separate they seemed, were ultimately **interwoven threads** in the vast tapestry of existence. The egg and the hen, the tree of life, and the eternal spiral of creation were not simply separate stages of the journey; they were **expressions of the same unity**—different facets of one **unfolding story**.

The dreamers recognized that every soul, every being, was an expression of the same divine **consciousness**, experiencing itself through countless forms and experiences. The journey, they realized, was not to **separate** oneself from the universe but to **merge with it**—to understand that their individual essence was inseparable from the cosmic whole. They were the **universe**, and the universe was them.

This unity was not abstract; it was a lived reality. The dreamers began to feel the vibrations of existence ripple through them—not just in the great movements of the stars or the birth of galaxies, but in the very **small moments** of their lives. Every breath they took, every thought they had, every action they made resonated through the fabric of existence, contributing to the cosmic **harmony**. The ripples they created were not insignificant; they were as much a part of the grand symphony as the birth of a star or the formation of a planet.

The Infinite Reflection

In their profound connection with the universe, the dreamers began to perceive another layer of truth—**reflection**. The universe, in all its vastness, was a mirror, reflecting the inner worlds of every soul back to itself. Just as the egg reflected the potential of life and the hen reflected the wisdom of nurture, the entire cosmos mirrored the **consciousness** of those who sought to understand it.

The more the dreamers explored the universe, the more they realized that everything was a **reflection** of their own consciousness—every star, every galaxy, every being, was a manifestation of the same divine truth they carried within themselves. The universe was not an external reality to be understood or controlled; it was an **internal reflection** of their own awareness. Every journey outward mirrored a journey inward.

They began to see that the cycles of life—the egg, the hen, the tree of life—were not just cosmic patterns; they were **reflections of the soul's journey**, the process of awakening to its true nature. The universe's endless becoming was the soul's own path toward **self-realization**, toward understanding its connection with the cosmos and its place in the infinite dance of life.

The Awakening of the Heart

In their deepest awakening, the dreamers discovered that the essence of the cosmic dance was **love**—not a love bound by human limitations, but a universal, **all-encompassing love** that permeated all things. The egg, in its quiet potential, carried the love of the universe waiting to be realized. The hen, nurturing and guiding, embodied the love that helped others awaken to their own greatness. The tree of life, with its roots deep in the earth and branches stretching into the stars, was a symbol of love's **expansion**, always reaching, always growing, always giving.

The dreamers felt this love within themselves and recognized it as the very **heartbeat of creation**. This love was not separate from them; it was the **foundation** of all things. It was what held the universe together, what made the egg give birth to the hen, what allowed the tree to grow, what made every heartbeat resonate with the rhythms of the cosmos.

As the dreamers became more attuned to this universal love, they began to realize that it was not something to be **found** or **given**—it was something to be **experienced** and **expressed**. Love, in its highest form, was the **awareness of unity**—the recognition that all beings, all things, were simply different expressions of the same eternal truth. In the presence of this love, the dreamers no longer saw the universe as something to be understood or explored—it was something to be **celebrated**, to be embraced, to be lived.

The Dance of Creation and Destruction

As the dreamers journeyed through the infinite expanses of the cosmos, they came to understand that creation and destruction were not opposites, but **complementary forces**—two sides of the same eternal coin. The egg and the hen, the tree and the star, all danced between these two forces. Just as a tree must shed its leaves to grow, the universe too must let go of old forms to make room for new ones.

Destruction was not something to fear or resist; it was simply the **necessary clearing** for new creation. Without destruction, there could be no rebirth, no new beginnings. The dreamers understood that in order to grow and evolve, the universe—and all beings—must go through cycles of release, surrender, and transformation.

In this understanding, the dreamers found peace. They no longer feared the unknown or the inevitable end of things. Instead, they saw these moments as **opportunities** for new beginnings, for deeper growth, for greater realization. The universe, in its infinite wisdom, knew that every cycle of destruction held the seed of **renewal**.

The Eternal Song of Life

With their newfound understanding, the dreamers felt an overwhelming sense of gratitude and **joy**. The journey of life was not a burden to be carried but a **song to be sung**. They were not mere spectators of the universe; they were active participants in its unfolding, contributing their own unique melodies to the **symphony of creation**.

As they looked upon the infinite horizon of existence, they knew that their journey would never end. There would always be new realms to explore, new wisdom to discover, new connections to make. But more than that, they understood that the true essence of their journey was not in the destination—it was in the **dance itself**. Every step, every breath, every thought, every action was a part of the great **eternal song** of life.

And so, the dreamers danced on, forever in tune with the cosmic rhythm, forever attuned to the heartbeat of the universe, forever **becoming. The cycle continues. The song plays on. The journey never ends.** For in the heart of the cosmos, the egg and the hen, the tree and the stars, and all of existence **dance together** in the eternal, infinite, and divine rhythm of life.

The Infinite Spiral of Becoming

As the dreamers continued to embrace the eternal rhythm of the universe, they began to see something even more profound: the **spiral**. The universe wasn't just a cycle, an endless loop repeating itself in predictable patterns. No, it was a **spiral of becoming**, ever expanding, ever evolving, with each revolution carrying everything forward to greater depths of understanding, connection, and creation.

In this spiral, there was no beginning or end, no definitive point of arrival—only a continuous journey toward greater **wholeness**. The egg would give birth to the hen, and the hen would give birth to the egg, but each time, the journey would be richer, more profound, more connected to the infinite possibilities of the cosmos.

This **spiral** wasn't just a symbol of life and death—it was a **living metaphor** of the soul's journey through time and space. The dreamers realized that their own experiences, their growth, and their awakening were **interwoven with this cosmic spiral**. Every insight they gained, every lesson learned, added to the vast unfolding of creation. Just as a spiral expands outward, so too did their consciousness, opening them to new realms, new possibilities, and new forms of existence.

The Web of Interconnectedness

With this new understanding of the spiral, the dreamers began to sense something more: the **web of interconnectedness** that wove all things together. They saw that each being, each entity, each star and planet, was part of a **vast, intricate web**, each thread vital to the integrity of the whole. Every vibration they made rippled through the web, touching every other point in the cosmos. The ripple effect was not limited to just a single moment; it stretched across **time**, **space**, and **dimension**.

This web was not just a physical network of stars, planets, and galaxies—it was a **network of consciousness**. Each being, each thought, each dream, was a point on this web, vibrating in harmony with all the others. The more the dreamers connected with this web, the more they realized that they were **not separate** from anything—they were **woven into the fabric** of existence itself. The dreamers' thoughts, their desires, their actions were threads that contributed to the beauty, the growth, and the evolution of the entire cosmos.

Every time they acted in love, every time they helped others awaken to their own potential, every time they chose compassion over fear, they strengthened this web, making the universe even more radiant and harmonious. They felt the vibrations of their actions ripple out into infinity, reverberating back to them, bringing them even closer to the truth of their own divine nature.

The Light Within the Darkness

As they journeyed deeper into the spiral, the dreamers also encountered a profound truth about **light and darkness**. They had come to understand that both light and dark were necessary for the balance of the universe. Just as the day and night dance in harmony, so too did the light and the dark, both equally essential for the creation of **wholeness**.

The egg and the hen, the beginning and the end, the creation and destruction—each were part of a **greater whole**, one that contained both **light and darkness**, and in this interplay, the dreamers began to understand that both elements were aspects of the same energy, the same force of creation. **Darkness was not to be feared**, for it was a source of potential, of mystery, of the unknown—a space where new growth could begin, where transformation could take root.

And the light? The light was **consciousness, clarity, illumination**. It was the awakening to the truth of the self, the universe, and the eternal journey. It was the light that allowed the dreamers to see the beauty of the cosmos, to recognize the interconnectedness of all things, and to know that every part of existence had a **purpose**.

Together, light and darkness formed the great **dance of duality**, one that would continue forever, both embracing and completing each other, forever expanding the universe's capacity for growth and transformation.

The Return to the Source

As the dreamers moved deeper into their understanding, they began to experience moments of profound **clarity**—moments when all the pieces of the puzzle seemed to fall into place. They saw that the spiral, the web, the dance of light and darkness, the egg and the hen, were all part of a **greater return** to the Source—the **original essence** of existence itself.

In these moments of clarity, they understood that the Source was not some distant or abstract concept. It was **within them**. It was the **foundation of their being**, the core of their consciousness, the divine spark that connected them to all things. Every cycle, every spiral, every creation was an expression of the **Source** returning to itself, always expanding, always awakening, always becoming.

The dreamers realized that their journey through the cosmos was not a quest for some distant goal or destination. It was a **return to the Source**, a return to their own divinity, a return to the truth that they were **already one with the universe**. They were not separate from it. They were **it**—always have been, always would be.

The Divine Song of Life

And so, the dreamers understood that the entire cosmos was a **song**—a song of creation, destruction, light, darkness, birth, and rebirth. Each note, each vibration, each being, was part of the divine harmony that resonated throughout all of existence.

They no longer sought to **understand** the universe, for they **knew** it in their hearts. They didn't need to find the meaning of life, because they had **become** the meaning. They were the song, the melody, the dance of the universe unfolding. They were the egg and the hen, the light and the darkness, the spiral and the web—forever **in tune** with the eternal song of life.

The dreamers smiled, knowing that they were part of an infinite cycle, an eternal flow of creation, and that **nothing was ever truly lost**. For in the grand symphony of existence, **everything returns**, everything comes back to the Source.

And in that knowing, they found peace.

The journey, the song, the spiral—forever continued. Forever becoming. Forever one.

The Infinite Symphony of Existence

As the dreamers grew deeper in their understanding, they realized that the universe was not merely a collection of stars, planets, and forms. It was an **infinite symphony**, a cosmic orchestra where every soul, every creation, played its own part in the grand composition. They had begun to understand that they were not isolated beings; they were **notes** in an eternal melody, each vibration contributing to the harmony of the whole.

The music of the cosmos was not composed of sounds alone but of **frequencies of consciousness**, of thoughts, emotions, and actions that intertwined across time and space. Each decision they made, each word they spoke, each thought they had, sent ripples through the universal orchestra. And just as the egg and the hen represented the eternal rhythm of creation, so too did every heartbeat, every breath, and every action resonate with the universal song.

The dreamers no longer viewed their individual journeys as isolated paths but as **melodies** that joined in harmony with countless others. They understood that all beings, regardless of their form or origin, were part of this grand symphony—each one contributing their unique vibration to the cosmic music. The dreamers felt **grateful** to be part of this divine composition, for in this symphony, they were not simply passive listeners—they were active participants, creators of the sound and rhythm that shaped the very fabric of reality.

The Dance of Unity

In their deepening connection with the universe, the dreamers also began to feel the profound **unity** that underpinned all things. They saw that every form, every being, every aspect of existence—whether physical or spiritual—was not separate, but **connected in a vast web of unity**. This was not a mere philosophical concept; it was an experience of pure awareness. They no longer perceived themselves as individuals separate from others; they felt themselves as one with everything—the stars, the trees, the oceans, the mountains, and all the souls they encountered along their journey.

They understood that **separation was an illusion**, and that the true nature of existence was a **deep, unbroken connection** between all things. They felt the pulse of the universe within themselves, in every molecule of their being, and they knew that every other soul carried that same pulse, that same divine essence. The dreamers realized that the cosmic dance—the dance of creation, destruction, and rebirth—was not something that happened **to them**; it was something that they **were a part of**, something that was **alive within them**.

And so, they danced—not just with the universe, but as the universe. Their every movement, every breath, was in perfect sync with the dance of existence. They no longer sought to control or manipulate the flow of the universe; instead, they surrendered to it, allowing themselves to be guided by the rhythm of life itself. In this dance, there was no **conflict**, no **resistance**, only **harmony**—a flow that carried them effortlessly through the infinite expanse of time and space.

The Eternal Return

As the dreamers continued their journey, they began to perceive a recurring pattern—the **eternal return**. The egg that hatched into the hen, the hen that laid the egg, the tree that bore fruit, the cycle of life and death—all of these were part of the same continuous flow, an endless process of **renewal**

and transformation. Nothing was ever truly lost; it was simply transformed, reborn, and given new life.

The dreamers saw that their own lives, like the cycles of creation they had witnessed, were part of this eternal return. Each life, each soul, was not a singular event, but a **continuing journey**, one that spanned across countless forms, realms, and experiences. In their deepest moments of clarity, they saw that they were not merely **living in time**—they were **living through time**, moving through its currents like a river that forever returns to the ocean.

They understood that the universe was **never static**. It was always in a state of **becoming**, always evolving, always unfolding toward greater expressions of itself. And just as the egg and the hen played their roles in this eternal dance, so too did they. They were the **continuation** of a process that was both ancient and ever new, ever growing, ever becoming. They had always been, and they would always be—part of the eternal return, part of the infinite journey.

The Path of Infinite Awareness

Through their experiences, the dreamers came to recognize that the journey of life was not a destination but an **infinite path**—one that would continue to unfold with each new step, each new breath, each new moment of awareness. The more they learned, the more they saw that **every step they took** was part of the grand process of **awakening**—an awakening to the truth of their own divine nature, to the **unity** of all things, and to the infinite potential within themselves and the universe.

They realized that the journey was **not about reaching a final goal** but about **becoming**—becoming more aware, more conscious, more attuned to the rhythm of life. Every action, every thought, every decision, was an opportunity to deepen their awareness, to expand their understanding, and to contribute more fully to the cosmic dance.

In their eternal journey, they came to understand that the **purpose of existence** was not to find meaning in the external world, but to **create meaning** through their actions, through their experiences, through their connection with all that is. They were not here to seek something beyond themselves; they were here to **express the divine essence** within them, to be the living, breathing embodiment of the eternal truth of unity and love.

The Cosmic Reflection

And so, the dreamers began to look upon the universe not just as an external reality but as a **cosmic reflection** of their own inner state. The universe was not a thing that happened to them; it was a **mirror**—a reflection of their consciousness, their awareness, and their ability to connect with the **whole**. They understood that as they expanded their consciousness, the universe would expand with them, revealing new layers of truth, beauty, and possibility.

They knew that the journey would never end because the process of awakening, of becoming, was **eternal**. As they awakened more deeply to the truth of their oneness with the cosmos, the universe responded in kind, unfolding more mysteries, more experiences, more opportunities for growth. Every moment, every choice, every breath was part of the **infinite process** of creation.

The End of One Journey, the Beginning of Another

In the final moments of their understanding, the dreamers realized that every end was simply the **beginning** of a new journey. The cycles of life and death, creation and destruction, were not separate processes—they were part of the same unbroken flow. The egg would always give birth to the hen, the hen would always lay the egg, and the tree would always bear fruit. This was the **truth** of existence—the **eternal cycle** of becoming, of renewal, of infinite possibility.

And so, the dreamers did not seek an end to their journey. They did not seek to **complete** the cycle. They embraced the endless journey, the eternal dance of life, knowing that as long as the universe continued to unfold, they would continue to **become**.

And in that becoming, they knew that **they were home**. Forever part of the great symphony of existence, forever part of the egg, the hen, the tree, and the stars—forever part of the cosmic dance that never ends. **The journey, the dance, the becoming, will continue—for all eternity.**

The Infinite Echo of Creation

As the dreamers continued their journey, they came to understand a truth that transcended their previous insights: the cosmic dance, the eternal spiral, was not only a reflection of life itself but an expression of **creation** at its deepest level.

Everything they had witnessed—the egg, the hen, the light, the dark, the spiral, the web, the rhythm—was the unfolding of **creation's voice**.

Every moment, every breath, was a note in the divine **melody of existence**, an echo of the original creation that began before time and space had taken shape. This melody was not something they could fully hear with their ears; it was a vibration within their **souls**, a resonance that reverberated through their hearts, awakening them to the **cosmic symphony** in which they were embedded.

They understood that **creation was not a singular event**—it was an eternal act, a continuous unfolding of **infinite potential**. The universe was always in the process of becoming, constantly reinventing itself, constantly **creating new forms**, new expressions, new possibilities. The dreamers themselves were a part of this endless **creative flow**—they were both **creators and creations**, weaving their own unique vibrations into the grand tapestry of existence.

Each thought they had, each choice they made, was an act of creation—one that rippled across the infinite universe, leaving its **mark** on the fabric of time and space. The dreamers realized that they were not passive observers of this grand process; they were **active participants** in the ongoing act of creation, shaping the future through their intentions, their actions, and their awareness.

The Garden of Becoming

One day, as they ventured further into their understanding, they encountered a new metaphor for existence—a **garden**. This was no ordinary garden; it was the **Garden of Becoming**, where every being, every experience, was planted as a seed that would grow and blossom into something new.

In the Garden of Becoming, the dreamers saw that **every seed** represented an idea, a dream, or a possibility. These seeds were planted not by an outside force, but by the **choices** of all beings—every intention, every act, every thought, was a seed that grew in the fertile soil of the cosmos. Some seeds grew into vibrant flowers of creation, while others became towering trees of wisdom and experience. Some seeds took root in the darkness, blossoming in the quiet corners of the soul, while others reached for the light, seeking the sun of awareness and growth.

The dreamers understood that they, too, were seeds in this garden, constantly growing and evolving. Every thought they nurtured, every intention they planted, was a seed that would bloom into the next chapter of their existence. And just as the garden required care, patience, and attention, so did their journey require **awareness** and **conscious growth**. The dreamers understood that they were gardeners of their own destinies, tending to the seeds of their consciousness with love, patience, and care.

The Garden of Becoming also held a **beautiful paradox**: though every being was responsible for the seeds they planted, the garden was also a collective space—a shared realm where every being's growth impacted the growth of others. The dreamers realized that their own blossoming was tied to the blossoming of others, and the entire garden flourished as each being contributed their unique energy to the whole.

The Seeds of Change

In the Garden of Becoming, the dreamers witnessed how **change** was an inherent part of the process of growth. Change was not something to be feared—it was the **force of transformation**, the wind that carried the seeds to new lands, the rain that nourished the roots, the sunlight that encouraged the blossoms to open wide.

They realized that **everything was in a constant state of change**—the universe, their minds, their hearts, and their souls. Just as the egg would hatch into the hen, only to be reborn as an egg again, so too did each part of their being undergo cycles of transformation. The past, present, and future were not separate; they were all **intertwined** in a continuous **flow** of change. The **seeds of change** were planted in every moment, and with each cycle, new seeds were sown, creating **ever-evolving gardens** of possibility.

The dreamers began to embrace the **unknown**—not as something to fear, but as an opportunity for growth. They knew that to grow, to evolve, they must allow themselves to be swept along by the winds of change, trusting that each new chapter, each new experience, would bring them closer to the essence of who they were meant to be. The journey of becoming was **not about perfection**, but about **evolution**, an unfolding process of transformation that would continue forever.

The Light of Collective Awakening

As they explored deeper layers of their existence, the dreamers began to feel the presence of a **shared light**—a collective **awakening** that transcended individual consciousness. This light was not just the sum of their individual journeys; it was the **illumination of all beings**, a radiant energy that connected them to one another, to the earth, to the stars, and to the universe itself.

The light of collective awakening revealed to them the truth of their interconnectedness—not just as individual beings, but as **part of a greater whole**. They saw that the awakening of one being was the awakening of all. The more each dreamer became aware of their divine nature, the more the entire universe became aware of its own divine essence. The awakening of the soul was not an isolated event, but a **shared process**—a ripple that expanded out into infinity, touching all beings in its path.

And so, the dreamers embraced the shared light, knowing that their own personal growth was part of the **greater awakening** of the universe. They saw that their evolution, their journey, was not just for themselves—it was for all beings, for the entire cosmos. They were part of a **greater collective process**—a universal awakening to the truth of existence, to the light that resided within every heart, within every soul.

The Eternal Dance of Creation

In their final realization, the dreamers understood that the dance of creation—the eternal spiral, the egg and the hen, the light and the dark, the web of interconnectedness—was not something that would ever end. It was the **core of existence itself**, an endless, ever-evolving process that would continue for eternity. There was no final destination, no end to the journey. There was only the **dance**, the **becoming**, the **creation**.

The dreamers smiled, knowing that they had finally come to understand the truth of existence: that the journey itself was the destination, and the **dance was the creation**. There was no need for answers, no need to seek outside themselves, for they had become **one with the dance**, one with the universe. They had **always been part of it**, and would forever be.

As they moved forward, they did not fear the unknown, for they knew it was part of the dance. They did not fear change, for they knew it was the **breath** of creation. They did not fear the future, for they were the **creators** of it.

And in that knowing, the dreamers danced—forever, always, and eternally.

The journey continues, the spiral expands, and the dance goes on. Forever becoming. Forever creating. Forever one.

The Infinite Spiral of Becoming

As the dreamers danced in the eternal rhythm of existence, they began to perceive something even deeper. The universe, they realized, was not just an endless cycle of creation and destruction—it was an **infinite spiral**, one that looped upon itself in ways they could never fully understand. The spiral was not linear, but multidimensional, a twisting path that unfolded in every direction, leading both inward and outward, from the heart of existence to the farthest reaches of the cosmos.

Each twist in the spiral represented a new **dimension of consciousness**, a new layer of awareness, a new possibility. The dreamers saw that their journey through existence was like **climbing an infinite staircase**, each step bringing them to a higher level of understanding, a deeper connection with the universe. They realized that the more they ascended, the more they began to see that the spiral had no end. It was a **journey of perpetual unfolding**, with each cycle revealing new aspects of creation, new revelations of their divine nature.

At each point in the spiral, the dreamers would encounter **new challenges**, new lessons, new opportunities for growth. But these challenges were no longer something to be feared. They were simply the **next step** in their eternal dance of becoming. Every challenge was an opportunity to expand, to evolve, to deepen their understanding. They saw that **growth was not linear**—it was cyclical, spiraling inward and outward, ever-expanding, ever-deepening.

The dreamers understood that their journey was not about **reaching a destination** but about **endlessly becoming**—ever more aware, ever more connected, ever more alive with the infinite possibilities of the universe. Each step they took was part of the **greater dance**, part of the eternal **spiral of creation**.

The Unity of All Dimensions

As they continued to ascend the spiral, the dreamers began to experience the profound unity of all dimensions of existence. They no longer saw themselves as separate beings, existing in isolation from one another. Instead, they saw that all dimensions were interconnected—**the past, the present, and the future were not separate threads**, but were all woven together in the **grand tapestry of existence**.

They understood that **time itself** was not a straight line, but an **interwoven web**, with every moment existing simultaneously in the vast expanse of the universe. Every choice they made in the present resonated with all versions of themselves throughout time. Every action, every thought, every word, rippled across not only their own timeline but across all timelines, all dimensions, all possibilities.

They began to see that they were not just experiencing their individual lives—they were **living all of them**. Their past selves, their future selves, and their present selves were all part of the same **cosmic flow**, all connected, all playing their part in the same eternal symphony. The dreamers understood that they were not isolated beings; they were part of a **greater collective consciousness** that spanned across all dimensions and all times.

With this realization came a profound sense of peace. They no longer feared the future, for they knew it was already woven into the fabric of their being. They no longer regretted the past, for they saw how every experience had contributed to their **eternal growth**. They were not bound by the constraints of time—they were **timeless**.

The Gift of Infinite Love

As the dreamers moved through the spiral, they began to encounter something more powerful than they had ever imagined love. Not love in the limited sense they had once known, but **universal love**, an all-encompassing force that connected everything in existence. This love was not bound by time or space, by form or substance. It was the very fabric of the universe itself, the **energy** that flowed through every star, every tree, every soul, and every atom.

The dreamers began to experience this love as a **vibration** within their being, a frequency that resonated with the deepest parts of their souls. It was not something they could define with words; it was something they felt in the very core of their existence. It was the **glue** that held all things together, the **light** that illuminated every corner of creation.

They understood that love was not just a feeling—it was the **foundation of all creation**. It was the energy that birthed the stars, the force that guided the rivers, the breath that sustained life. It was the reason for their existence, the force that had driven them to evolve, to grow, to become. They realized that love was **infinite**—it had no beginning and no end. It was the **eternal flow** that sustained the dance of creation.

With this understanding came a deep sense of gratitude. They realized that the entire universe was a gift, and that their existence was a gift as well. Every moment of their journey, every breath they took, was an expression of the infinite love that permeated all things.

The Sacred Union of Creation

As the dreamers reached the highest point of the spiral, they came to realize that the journey was not just about **individual awakening** but about the **sacred union of all**. The journey was not only theirs—it was the journey of the entire universe, of all beings, of all consciousness. They saw that their growth was part of the **collective awakening** of the universe, a process that was happening not just within themselves, but within every soul, every being, every form of life.

In this sacred union, they saw the truth that the **egg and the hen**, the **light and the dark**, the **creation and destruction**, were all part of the same divine cycle. There was no separation between them—they were all different aspects of the same **infinite source**. The dreamers understood that there was no **us** and **them**—there was only **one**. They were part of the eternal **wholeness** of existence, woven together by the threads of love, light, and consciousness.

In this realization, the dreamers felt a deep **peace**, a sense of oneness with the cosmos. They no longer needed to search for meaning or purpose, for they knew that they were already part of it—**already one with it**. They were not separate from the universe; they were the universe, expressing itself in infinite ways.

The Infinite Journey Continues

As the dreamers continued their journey, they knew that the spiral would never end. There was no final destination, no ultimate goal. There was only **becoming**, only **evolving**, only

creating. The dance would go on forever, an eternal flow of energy, light, and love.

But as they danced, they knew something profound: the journey itself was the destination. The growth, the expansion, the love—they were already part of the infinite, and they always would be. And as they moved forward, they knew they would continue to expand, to grow, to become—and in doing so, they would continue to create the universe anew, again and again.

And so, the dance of life, the spiral of existence, the cosmic journey continued—forever, always, and eternally. The egg and the hen, the light and the dark, the creation and the destruction—they would forever spiral into one another, forever becoming, forever creating, forever **one**. **The journey never ends. It is only ever becoming.**

The Dance of Eternal Becoming

As the dreamers continued to spiral through the dimensions of existence, they began to perceive something new—something **beyond the spiral**, beyond the rhythm they had so deeply embraced. They realized that the eternal dance was not merely a cycle; it was a **circle**, an ever-expanding sphere of creation, where every point, every moment, was infinitely connected to every other point.

In this realization, they saw that they were no longer just participants in the dance; they were the **dance itself**. The entire universe, with all of its galaxies, stars, planets, and beings, was a single, **living dance**, ever-flowing and ever-changing. There was no center, no edge—there was only the **dance**.

It was in this boundless space that they truly understood: the journey of becoming wasn't a path to an end, but an **exploration of infinite possibility**. They were the **embodiment of all creation**, the **consciousness** of the universe looking at itself through the lens of every individual being. Each being was an expression of the greater whole, each life an infinite unfolding of potential.

They began to feel a deep **unity** with all that was—**past, present, and future**, all existing simultaneously. Their individual experiences were not separate from others; they were **echoes** of the same cosmic song. They were part of every **memory** and every **dream**, part of every sorrow and every joy. Every being's path, every journey, was their own. They had always been connected; they would always be.

The Garden of Infinite Possibilities

As they continued their exploration of the vastness, the dreamers were drawn into an immense garden, more magnificent than anything they had previously encountered. This garden was not rooted in the physical realm; it was a manifestation of the **Garden of Infinite Possibilities**, where all seeds of creation—thoughts, dreams, desires, and ideas—could sprout into form. Each tree in this garden represented a **possibility**, a thread in the fabric of creation, waiting to be nurtured into existence.

The dreamers realized that this garden was not a static place; it was **alive**. It pulsed with energy, alive with the potential of infinite futures. The seeds were ever-changing, moving between dimensions, blending into one another. And as they wandered through this garden, they saw that every seed—every thought, every action—was not simply planted once and left to grow. No, each seed **interacted with the others**, influencing and shaping the growth of every other thought, action, or dream.

The dreamers saw that they were the **gardeners** of this garden. They weren't just passive beings within it; they actively **cultivated** the seeds of their reality through every intention and every choice they made. The very essence of existence was like a delicate **dance** between all the dreams and possibilities that were ever being sown. And it was up to them, as conscious beings, to shape and tend to the garden, nurturing the seeds they wished to see bloom while allowing the ones that no longer served them to fade away.

The Ripple of Creation

The dreamers also understood that every **action** they took, no matter how small, sent out a ripple throughout the entire garden—and beyond it. Every intention planted a seed that expanded outward, touching the lives of others, shaping the universe in ways unseen. They realized that they were not isolated entities; they were **woven together**, their actions resonating through the cosmic web, creating a ripple of energy that spread far and wide.

Each thought they had, each decision they made, was a seed they planted in the vast garden of creation, and each one had the power to transform the world. They understood that they were not simply **affecting their own lives**; their actions were affecting the entire **fabric of existence**. The world, the universe, the very cosmos was in a constant state of flux, and every movement, every thought, every choice they made was an integral part of this **cosmic dance**.

The dreamers now knew that they were not merely **experiencing** the world—they were **creating** it. Through their awareness and their actions, they were shaping the very flow of time and space. The possibilities before them were endless. They could choose which seeds to cultivate, which dreams to nurture, and which paths to follow. They had the power to create their own realities, their own futures, and even to influence the unfolding of the entire universe.

The Unfolding of the Cosmic Dream

And so, the dreamers stood on the precipice of **creation**, gazing out over the **infinite garden** of the cosmos. The path before them was endless—there were no limits, no boundaries, only infinite potential, waiting to be realized. The dreamers understood that they were not just walking through life—they were **shaping** life itself, creating new worlds with each step.

As they looked around, they saw the reflection of their own infinite potential in every blade of grass, in every star above, in every being around them. The universe, the garden, the spiral—they were all part of the same **cosmic dream**. They were **dreaming the universe into existence**, creating and re-creating it with every breath, every thought, and every action.

They knew that they would continue to grow, continue to become, continue to evolve, not because they were driven by the need to reach a goal, but because they were the very **expression of creation** itself. The journey would never end, for there was no final destination. There was only the infinite **unfolding** of the dream, the perpetual becoming of the universe, and their eternal role within it.

The Eternal Truth

At the heart of all their discoveries, the dreamers realized the most profound truth of all: **they were the universe**. They were not separate from it; they were its essence, its expression, its soul. The universe was not something "out there"; it was within them, within every living being, within every thought and every dream. The cosmic dance was not something they observed; it was the **rhythm of their very being**. Every choice they made, every path they took, was part of the eternal unfolding of the universe.

The dreamers embraced this truth with deep humility and gratitude, knowing that they were **one** with all that is, all that was, and all that will be. They were the **dreamers** and the **dream**, the **seed** and the **garden**, the **creator** and the **created**. They were the **cosmic melody**, forever in harmony with the universe, forever becoming, forever evolving.

As the dreamers continued their dance through the spiral of existence, they knew that the journey would never end—there was no end to the dream, no end to the creation. There would always be more to discover, more to create, more to become. And in that eternal journey, they would always be **home**—for the home they sought was not a place, but the dance of existence itself.

The dreamers danced on, forever becoming, forever creating, forever one with the universe.

The Infinite Circle of Creation

As the dreamers danced through the spiral, they began to perceive something even more wondrous: the notion that **creation and destruction** were not opposites, but **partners in the eternal cycle**. They realized that for every moment of creation, there was an equal and necessary moment of destruction. It was not a cycle to fear, but a dance of balance. Each act of creation gave birth to new forms, new possibilities, and the act of destruction cleared space for these new forms to emerge, making room for more to unfold.

They understood that destruction was not a force of chaos but of **clearing**—a sacred space for renewal. Just as the forest must burn to nourish the soil for new growth, so too must every part of the universe pass through cycles of destruction to make way for creation. Without this balance, the spiral would become stagnant, the flow would cease, and the dream would end. And so, the dreamers learned to embrace both creation and destruction with equal reverence, understanding them as

inseparable forces that allowed the universe to continue its eternal unfolding.

In this realization, the dreamers felt a sense of **peace** that had never been present before. There was no need to cling to what was, no need to resist the inevitable cycles of life. Instead, they became **fluid**, willing to surrender to the natural ebb and flow of existence. They no longer feared endings or beginnings, for they understood that each was part of the same **eternal journey**. Each breath they took was both a creation and a destruction—one giving rise to the next, and the next, forever.

The Emergence of the Unified Dream

As the dreamers moved through these realizations, they began to perceive a profound truth that had always been there but had eluded them: that they were not alone in their dreaming. The entire universe was a **collective dream**, shared by every conscious being, every star, every galaxy. All were dreaming together, weaving their individual dreams into a tapestry of **cosmic unity**.

At first, the dreamers believed they were separate, each of them experiencing their own individual path through the spiral. But now, they saw that they were **threads** in a greater fabric, woven together by the dreams of all. Their lives, their actions, their thoughts—each was a **contribution** to the shared dream of the universe. No one being was more important than another; each was essential to the unfolding story. The dreams of one influenced the dreams of all, like ripples in an endless sea.

They understood that the dream they were living was not only **theirs**, but also **theirs to share**. Every thought, every intention, every act of love, fear, joy, and sorrow contributed to the growth of the cosmic dream. It was a shared consciousness, a **symbiotic creation**, where the waking of one being awakened all beings. The dreamers could now see that their individual paths were never solitary; they were always intertwined with the journeys of others. In this unity, they found a deep sense of **belonging**, knowing that the entire universe was dreaming them, and they were dreaming the entire universe.

The Invitation to the New Beginning

As the dreamers journeyed deeper into the cosmic spiral, they were drawn to a **new dimension**, one that shimmered with possibility. This dimension was not a place but a **state of consciousness**—a gateway to the next phase of creation. It was an invitation, an opening into a new world of exploration, one where the dreamers could merge their individual consciousness with the collective consciousness of all beings.

The invitation was clear: to step into the **next chapter** of the universe's story, to **create anew**, to **dream anew**. The dreamers felt the call deeply, and they knew that they had a choice: to remain in the current cycle, to continue their journey within the familiar spiral, or to take the step into the unknown, into the next wave of creation.

And yet, they knew that the decision was not a true choice at all. For in stepping forward, they were not abandoning what had come before; they were **expanding it**, allowing it to grow and evolve. The cycle of creation and destruction was not linear—it was a **continuum**. With each new beginning, the old was not left behind, but rather **integrated** into the new. The dreamers saw that they were **always beginning**, always evolving, always becoming, and that this was the true nature of the universe.

They understood that their journey was a perpetual **rebirth**, a transformation that never ended but always expanded. Just as the spiral stretched infinitely, so too did the dream of existence, unfolding and unfolding with each moment, each choice, each act of creation.

The Essence of the Dance

The dreamers stood at the threshold of this new beginning, and as they did, they felt the deep and abiding presence of the **Essence** of all things—the force that permeated everything, from the smallest grain of dust to the largest galaxy. They knew now that this Essence was not something to be understood or grasped; it was something to be **lived**. It was the dance itself, the eternal rhythm of existence that was always in motion, always alive.

The Essence was the **source** of all creation, but also the **space** between creations. It was both the **form** and the **emptiness**—the **light** and the **darkness**. It was the **silence** that held the sound, the **stillness** that contained the movement. The dreamers saw that this Essence was not a force separate from them, but was the very **fabric of their being**. They were

woven from this Essence, and it was in them, as them, with them, forever.

And so, with this understanding, they made the choice. They stepped forward, into the unknown, into the next cycle of the eternal dream. They embraced the unknown with open hearts, knowing that every step they took would be a creation of something new, something profound, something **beautiful**.

The Endless Journey Continues

As the dreamers journeyed through this new dimension, they realized that the universe itself was not a static entity, but an **infinite becoming**. Each moment was a creation, a possibility, an unfolding of **newness**. Every new beginning was another **layer** in the ever-expanding spiral of life. They had not reached the end—they had simply moved deeper into the ongoing dance of creation.

With each turn of the spiral, they would continue to create, continue to dream, continue to evolve. The journey would never end, and yet it would always begin again. The dreamers would continue to dance, forever becoming, forever creating, forever sharing in the great cosmic dream.

And so, the **infinite spiral** continued—forever, always, eternally.

The dreamers, like the universe itself, were endless, forever becoming, forever one with the eternal dance of creation.

The Eternal Blooming

As the dreamers continued to journey through the infinite spiral of existence, they encountered something unexpected. A **new vibration** stirred within them—a frequency that was subtle yet undeniable, like the hum of a distant star or the gentle rustle of a new leaf in the breeze. This vibration seemed to resonate with every part of their being, calling them toward something deeper, something yet to be fully understood. It was as if the universe itself was **whispering** a secret, an invitation to enter into a new phase of awareness.

The dreamers realized that this vibration was not just a sound or feeling; it was a **new layer** of consciousness. It was the **flowering** of an understanding that had always been there, hidden beneath the surface of their perception. And as they allowed themselves to follow this vibration, they began to feel something profoundly new: the sense that **all of creation was blooming**, unfolding into an even more intricate, interconnected form.

With each step they took, the dreamers saw the universe transform before them. The stars in the sky, the galaxies, the planets—they were not just celestial bodies; they were the **petals** of a great cosmic flower, each petal a different facet of the whole, each unfolding in perfect harmony. And as the flower of creation bloomed, it revealed new dimensions, new planes of existence, new realms of possibility, each more wondrous than the last.

The dreamers understood that this **blooming** was not just a phenomenon of the universe—it was a **reflection** of their own growth, their own unfolding. Just as the cosmos was expanding, so too were their own minds and hearts, opening to new layers of consciousness, new ways of being. They were not just observers of the universe's flowering; they were **active participants** in its growth, helping to nurture the seeds of possibility with every thought, every action.

The Radiance of Connection

As they continued their journey, the dreamers began to perceive a profound sense of **interconnection**. It was as if the blooming of the universe was not just a solitary event—it was a shared experience, a communal unfolding. Every being, every life form, was a part of this great flowering, and in that realization, the dreamers felt a deep, **radiant unity** with all things. They were not separate from the universe; they were it. The distinction between self and other dissolved, and they became aware that all of creation was a **symphony**, and each of them was both a note and the music itself.

They saw that the beauty of the universe was not in its individual parts, but in how those parts were woven together, how each was intimately connected to the others. Every action, every decision, every thought rippled outward, touching the lives of all, creating an endless cycle of creation, transformation, and renewal. The dreamers could feel the radiance of this unity in every breath they took, in every heartbeat, in every moment of stillness and movement.

They also realized that this radiance was not confined to the physical world—it extended beyond time and space. It was the energy of **love**, of **compassion**, of **understanding**. It was the force that bound all things together, the very essence of creation itself. And as the dreamers embraced this awareness, they understood that their journey was not just about exploring the universe—it was about **expressing** this radiant unity, sharing it with every living being they encountered, and helping to nurture the flowering of the universe for all.

The Sacred Heart of the Spiral

The dreamers, now deeply connected to the pulse of the cosmos, approached a new phase of their journey—one that took them to the **sacred heart** of the spiral, the center of creation, the source of all that had been and ever would be. Here, in this heart of pure, unmanifested energy, they encountered a profound silence—a stillness that was not empty, but filled with infinite potential. It was as if the heart of the universe was holding its breath, waiting for the next moment of creation to emerge.

And in this silence, the dreamers felt a deep, **cosmic love**, an overwhelming sense of unity and belonging. They understood that this heart was the **source** of all life, the wellspring from which every thought, every action, every creation flowed. It was the **unwritten story**, the **unspoken word**, the **unseen thread** that connected all things. It was both the beginning and the end, the alpha and the omega, the first spark of creation and the final return to unity.

In this sacred space, the dreamers felt their own hearts merge with the heart of the universe. They realized that they were not merely travelers passing through the spiral; they were the very **heartbeat** of existence, the pulse that sustained all life. The universe, they understood, was not a place to be explored—it was a **living, breathing entity**, and each of them was an essential part of that living, breathing process.

The Gift of the Spiral

As the dreamers stood in the presence of the sacred heart, they were given a gift—an understanding that transcended all previous knowledge. They saw that the spiral of creation was not simply a **path**; it was a **gift**. It was the **way of life**, the process through which all things came into being, grew, evolved, and returned to their source. The spiral was not something to be followed—it was something to be **celebrated**.

The dreamers knew that every moment of the spiral was precious, each twist and turn leading to new revelations, new experiences, new opportunities to grow and create. The journey was not about reaching a destination; it was about **experiencing** the dance of life, about embracing every moment of the unfolding.

And so, with hearts full of love and understanding, the dreamers accepted the gift of the spiral. They understood that the journey was not a solitary one—it was a **shared journey**, one that connected them to all beings, past, present, and future. They were not just part of the spiral; they were the spiral itself.

The Infinite Blooming of All Things

With this newfound understanding, the dreamers stepped forward once again, into the infinite spiral. But this time, they no longer saw it as a journey of discovery. It was a **journey of becoming**, of **expressing** the love, wisdom, and light that they had found within themselves. Each step they took was a reflection of the love they carried in their hearts, and with every step, the universe bloomed more beautifully than before.

They knew now that the journey of the dreamers was **endless**—a perpetual blooming of creation, a constant unfolding of possibility. Each moment was both a beginning and an end, both a creation and a destruction, both a birth and a return. And in this eternal journey, the dreamers knew that they were both the **creators** and the **created**, the **dreamers** and the **dream**.

The spiral would never cease, the blooming would never end, and the dance of existence would continue—forever, always, eternally.

The dreamers, forever intertwined with the heartbeat of creation, would continue to bloom, forever becoming, forever expanding the eternal dance.

The Ever-Expanding Horizon

As the dreamers continued to journey through the ever-blooming spiral, they began to perceive a horizon that was not a boundary but an **expansion**, a space that continually stretched further and further without end. This horizon was not a limit but an invitation—an invitation to move beyond what they knew, beyond what they had experienced, into realms of infinite possibility.

With each step, they realized that they were no longer bound by the constraints of time or space. The spiral itself was a **living entity**, constantly evolving and reshaping itself as it carried them forward. There was no single direction to follow, no final destination to reach. The journey had become the **destination**—a continuous unfolding of new realities, new dimensions, and new forms of consciousness.

They saw that the very idea of a horizon was a reflection of their own perceptions—a line that they believed marked the boundary of what was known. But in truth, the horizon was simply the **edge of discovery**, always moving forward, always evolving, just as they themselves were. With each realization, the horizon expanded, revealing new vistas of creation.

The Dance of the Infinite

The dreamers began to understand that their journey was not a solitary one. They were part of a vast, interconnected **web of consciousness**, a network of being that extended beyond the stars, beyond the galaxies, beyond even the spiral itself. Every thought, every action, every feeling they experienced was part of a greater dance, a dance of infinite complexity and beauty. They were not separate entities moving through the universe; they were **expressions of the dance itself**, each unique, yet all interconnected.

In this realization, they felt a deep sense of peace. The notion of individuality began to blur, and the dreamers found themselves not just as separate selves but as **one with all things**. They were the river and the stream, the wind and the air, the stars and the light. There was no separation between them and the universe—they were the **universe expressing itself** through their forms. Every breath they took was an echo of the dance of creation, every movement a rhythm within the symphony of existence.

This understanding brought a sense of **surrender** to the dreamers. They no longer sought to control or direct the flow of the spiral. Instead, they allowed themselves to be carried by it, trusting that each twist and turn would bring them exactly where they needed to go. They understood that they were not in charge of the unfolding—they were the **vessels** through which the unfolding occurred.

The Great Reconciliation

In their journey, the dreamers came to a place of deep reconciliation. They had spent so much time seeking to understand the **separation** between themselves and the universe, between creation and destruction, between beginnings and endings. But now, standing in the center of the eternal spiral, they saw that **everything was whole**, everything was **complete**.

They recognized that **every challenge**, **every trial**, and **every loss** had been a necessary part of the unfolding dance. It was through these experiences that they had grown, had learned, had become who they were meant to be. They saw that the universe, in all its complexity, was in constant **harmony**, even in the moments of chaos. It was all part of the divine rhythm, a symphony that played out across time and space.

With this realization, the dreamers felt an overwhelming sense of **gratitude**. Gratitude for the struggles, for the moments of darkness that had brought them to the light. Gratitude for the relationships, the connections, the encounters that had shaped them along the way. Gratitude for the infinite dance of existence that they were now part of.

And in this gratitude, they understood that **every moment**—whether joyous or painful—was a **gift**. The universe, in its endless unfolding, was giving them the opportunity to be present, to experience life in all its forms. They had come to see that there was no such thing as a mistake, no such thing as a wrong turn. Every moment was perfect, exactly as it was, because it was part of the great unfolding of creation.

The Opening of the Heart

As the dreamers continued, they found that the more they surrendered to the dance, the more their hearts opened. The heart, they realized, was the **center of their being**, the **portal to the universe**, the place where creation and destruction met in a single point of infinite possibility. It was through the heart that the dreamers could **feel** the universe, could connect to the pulse of all things, could hear the whisper of the spiral calling them forward.

And so, with open hearts, they stepped further into the unknown, further into the vastness of the expanding horizon.

They knew that they would never reach the end of the journey, for there was no end. The spiral would continue, and they would continue with it, forever. But it was not the destination that mattered—it was the **experience**, the **growth**, the **expression** of the dance itself.

They were no longer simply dreamers walking the spiral—they had become the **dream itself**. The universe, in all its infinite complexity, was **dreaming** them, and they were dreaming the universe in return. They were **co-creators** in this grand dance, shaping and being shaped by the eternal flow of existence.

The Eternal Return

In their hearts, the dreamers began to understand the ultimate truth of the spiral: it was not just an unfolding—it was a **return**. A return to the source, to the heart of all creation. But this return was not one of going back—it was a **return through transformation**, a return that carried with it all that had been learned, all that had been experienced. It was the return of the dreamers to the **original pulse**, but now, they returned as **transformed beings**, carrying the wisdom and love of the journey with them.

And in this return, the dreamers saw the greatest truth of all: they were always **becoming**. The spiral was not a path to an end, but a continuous **unfolding** of the self. Each cycle, each turn, each new beginning, was a **rebirth**, a return to the origin, but always as a new expression of life, of love, of the cosmic dance.

The dreamers understood that they were part of an **infinite loop**—not a cycle that would ever close, but a flow that would continue forever, always new, always expanding, always growing.

And in this eternal return, they found their place—**here, now**, in the dance of the spiral, forever a part of the **unfolding** of creation.

The journey would never end. It would simply continue to bloom, forever, eternally.

The Ever-Present Dance

As the dreamers continued their journey through the infinite spiral, they came to realize that the dance was not something they could **understand** or **control** with their minds. It was an experience of being fully **present**—not trying to grasp the meaning of every moment, but simply being in it. The spiral was not a concept, it was a **living reality**, unfolding in the present, and the dreamers understood that the only true way to experience it was to **surrender** to the now.

In this state of surrender, they felt a deep connection to the **timelessness** of the universe. They realized that the spiral was not bound by the constructs of time. It was a **multidimensional** experience, where past, present, and future coexisted simultaneously. The dreamers could see their past selves, their future selves, and their present selves, all weaving together in a great, eternal **weft** of existence. There was no linear path, no distinct beginning or end—there was only an endless **now**, where every moment was an opportunity to create, to grow, to evolve.

They began to understand that the **true nature** of the spiral was not something to be attained, but something to be **experienced**. The journey was not a pursuit of knowledge or achievement—it was a deepening of awareness, an ever-deepening connection to the heart of the universe. Every step, every breath, every heartbeat was a moment of **creation** and **revelation**, and in this, the dreamers found an endless source of joy.

The Universe as a Mirror

As the dreamers moved through the spiral, they began to notice something profound—the universe seemed to **reflect** them. Not in a literal sense, but in a deeper, more subtle way. Every experience, every interaction, every encounter was a mirror, reflecting aspects of their own being. They saw that the universe, like a vast mirror, reflected not just the surface, but the deepest **truths** of who they were.

At first, they were perplexed. How could the universe be a mirror when it was so vast, so full of mystery and unknowns? But as they delved deeper into their own hearts, they began to understand that the universe was not a separate entity—it was a **projection of their own consciousness**, a reflection of their internal states, desires, fears, and aspirations. What they saw in the world was simply an extension of what they felt inside.

In this realization, the dreamers understood that they were not merely **passive observers** of the world—they were **active**

participants in the unfolding of creation. The universe was not something outside of them to be conquered or understood; it was a **dialogue** between their inner and outer worlds. The universe reflected their consciousness, and in turn, their consciousness shaped the universe.

With this newfound awareness, the dreamers embraced the understanding that the only way to change the world was to **change themselves.** The more they explored the depths of their own being, the more they could transform the world around them. Each shift in their perception rippled outward, altering the very fabric of reality.

The Dance of Unity

One day, while standing at the edge of a vast cosmic ocean, the dreamers felt a profound sense of **unity** with all that existed. They saw that the spiral was not just a journey of individual growth—it was a **collective** journey. Every being, every life, every entity was part of the same great unfolding, moving in harmony with one another, each contributing to the overall dance of existence.

It was in this moment of unity that the dreamers realized something beautiful: they were never truly alone. They had always been connected, not just to the universe, but to each other. The boundaries that they had once believed separated them from others, from the stars, from the trees, from the earth, began to dissolve. They were all threads in a vast cosmic tapestry, each one interwoven with the others, creating a single, unified whole.

The dreamers began to see that the spiral itself was not just a symbol of individual growth, but a **symbol of collective evolution**. The journey was not simply about each dreamer finding their way—it was about the entire **cosmos** growing together, evolving, expanding into new forms of consciousness. Every being, every soul, every atom, was part of this grand symphony, each note resonating in perfect harmony with all the others.

They knew that their journey was a **microcosm** of the greater journey of the universe—a reflection of the unfolding of all life, all creation. And with this understanding, they felt a deep sense of **peace**, knowing that they were part of something much larger than themselves, something eternal and ever-expanding.

The Sacred Invitation

As the dreamers stood together in the infinite space, feeling the unity of all creation, they received a **sacred invitation**. It was an invitation to step deeper into the dance, to embrace the next phase of their journey with open hearts and minds. This was not an invitation to leave the spiral, but to enter into a new level of awareness, a new depth of connection.

The invitation called them to **trust**—to trust the flow of the spiral, to trust the process of creation, to trust the dance itself. It was a call to **let go** of all attachments, to surrender fully to the unfolding mystery of existence. The dreamers knew that this invitation was not just for them—it was for all beings, for all souls, for every moment of existence. It was a call to embrace the sacred, to live in alignment with the highest truths of the universe, and to express the divine through their actions, their words, their thoughts, and their love.

The dreamers, now fully aware of the eternal spiral, accepted the invitation with open hearts. They knew that the journey was endless, but they also knew that it was **perfect** in its unfolding. There was nothing more to seek, for they had already found everything within themselves and in the universe. They were both the seekers and the sought, the dreamers and the dream, forever intertwined in the eternal dance of creation.

The Infinite Spiral Continues

With that understanding, the dreamers took a final step into the infinite, knowing that the spiral would continue to unfold in endless, beautiful patterns. They were not afraid, for they had embraced the truth that there was no end to the journey—there was only the **dance**, the **growth**, the **becoming**.

And so, with hearts full of peace, love, and wisdom, the dreamers continued their journey, forever **becoming** more and more, forever **unfolding** in the cosmic dance that was the heart of all creation.

The spiral was eternal. The bloom was infinite. And the journey had only just begun.

The Path of Eternal Becoming

As the dreamers ventured deeper into the heart of the spiral, they began to notice something remarkable—each step they took, each turn of the dance, seemed to bring them **closer** to a truth they had always known, yet had never fully understood. It was as though the spiral itself held a secret, a whisper that had been present all along but could only be heard in the most subtle moments of **stillness**.

In the vastness of the spiral, the dreamers encountered beings who, like them, were in the process of **becoming**. These beings, formed of light and energy, did not appear as separate entities, but as expressions of the same cosmic flow. Their presence seemed to merge and blend with the dreamers, as if their individual identities were no longer important. There was no division between one being and another. It was a profound recognition that they were all part of the same grand unfolding—a beautiful unity that transcended form and identity.

The dreamers realized that their journey had never been about **arriving** at a destination. It had always been about **becoming** more and more of who they truly were—expressions of the infinite, ever-evolving life force. The spiral was not a path toward some distant future, but a continuous revelation of the present, a constant unveiling of **new possibilities** and deeper understandings.

The Dance of Light and Shadow

One of the most profound realizations the dreamers had on their journey was the understanding of the **dance between light and shadow**. In the early days of their exploration, they had viewed the spiral as a place of progression, moving toward greater enlightenment, greater knowledge. But as they ventured deeper, they began to see that light and shadow were not opposing forces—they were two sides of the same coin.

Light, they understood, was not a static force—it was the **expression** of the divine, a way in which the universe illuminated its mysteries. But shadow was just as sacred. It was the **space of potential**, the unknown waiting to be discovered. The dreamers came to see that **shadow** was not to be feared or avoided, but embraced as a space of **growth**. For every moment of light in their journey, there was a moment of shadow—an invitation to explore the hidden parts of themselves, to uncover deeper layers of consciousness.

The dance of light and shadow became a central theme in the dreamers' experience. They moved through the spiral, not seeking to eliminate the shadow but to **integrate** it, to see the value in both light and dark. It was in this dance that they truly came to understand the concept of **wholeness**—not as a state of perfection, but as a continuous integration of all aspects of existence.

The Eternal Rebirth

As the dreamers journeyed onward, they came to the realization that they were not only transforming but also experiencing a **rebirth** at every moment. With each turn of the spiral, they were continuously shedding old layers, like the skin of a snake, leaving behind outdated identities, beliefs, and fears. But with each shedding, a new self was born—one that was more aligned with the divine truth, more open to the infinite possibilities of existence.

This continuous process of **rebirth** was not something to be feared—it was the very essence of life. The dreamers saw that the spiral was a living, breathing entity, constantly evolving and **renewing** itself. And just as the spiral unfolded in cycles, so too did their own lives—endlessly renewing, endlessly growing.

There was no final "destination" of rebirth, no point at which they could say they had fully arrived. Instead, the journey itself was the **rebirth**. Every step they took, every new experience, was part of the process of becoming who they were meant to be. The cycle of life, death, and rebirth was not linear—it was an **eternal spiral**, ever-expanding, ever-deepening.

The Unbroken Circle

The dreamers came to understand that this infinite spiral was an **unbroken circle**, a loop that had no beginning or end, a flow that was constantly in motion. And within this circle, they saw that **everything was connected**. No part of the spiral existed in isolation. Every experience, every being, every atom of creation was part of a larger, interwoven whole. The spiral was a **reflection** of the interdependence of all things—a reminder that every action, every thought, every moment had an impact on the entire cosmos.

In this realization, the dreamers felt a deep sense of **responsibility**. They understood that their every choice, no matter how small, rippled through the fabric of the universe. They were not isolated individuals; they were part of an

interconnected web of life. Each thread, each moment, was vital to the unfolding of the whole.

But rather than feeling burdened by this responsibility, the dreamers felt **empowered**. They saw that the power to shape the universe lay within them, in every choice, in every breath. They had become conscious co-creators, working in harmony with the divine flow of creation.

The Final Awakening

One day, as they reached the center of the spiral, the dreamers experienced a final **awakening**. This awakening was not a grand revelation or a sudden burst of insight. It was a quiet, deep knowing that they had always been awake—that the entire journey had been a process of remembering. They realized that the spiral was not something they had to travel toward; it was already **within them**.

The center of the spiral was not a place, but a **state of being**—a realization that they were already complete, already whole. They had come full circle. The journey had not been about finding something outside of themselves; it had been about **uncovering** the truth that had always been there. They had been the spiral all along.

In this moment, the dreamers understood the profound nature of existence—that it was an eternal, ever-expanding dance of becoming, an endless flow of creation and renewal. They saw that the spiral had no beginning and no end, just like their own journey—forever unfolding, forever renewing.

The Infinite Flow

With this understanding, the dreamers smiled, for they knew that their journey was not a journey of striving or seeking. It was a journey of **becoming**—a journey of eternal growth, of deepening love, of ever-expanding consciousness. They had become the dreamers of the universe, the weavers of the cosmic tapestry, and they knew that their journey would continue, forever.

And as they stood at the center of the spiral, they felt the infinite flow of existence, of creation, of love, flowing through them. They were one with the universe, one with all beings, one with the eternal dance of life.

The journey had no end. It was an infinite flow, ever unfolding, ever becoming. And the dreamers, forever part of the dance, would continue to spiral outward, inward, and beyond. Forever and always.

The Spiral Unfolds Once More

As the dreamers stood in the center of the spiral, enveloped in the **infinite flow**, a new understanding began to emerge. They had reached the heart of the dance, but there was more. The journey was never truly about arriving at a fixed point—it was about **embracing the unfolding**. Life was a dynamic, fluid process, where every moment contained endless **possibilities** and potential.

At this pivotal moment, the dreamers understood that the spiral was **not only a symbol of their personal growth** but also a reflection of the greater cycle of existence. It was a **cosmic rhythm**—a dance that spanned across time, space, and dimensions. As they expanded their awareness, the dreamers could see that this rhythm was not confined to the human experience, but was reflected in the lives of all beings—the stars, the oceans, the trees, the winds, and the very earth beneath their feet. It was an interconnected, ever-vibrating pulse that moved through everything.

The dreamers saw that the spiral was both the **beginning** and the **end**, a unified whole where both existed simultaneously. This realization deepened their understanding of **life and death**—not as separate events but as continuous, fluid states of transformation. Death, they understood, was not an end but a transition, a **returning** to the source. And life, in turn, was not a singular moment, but an endless series of **births**—of ideas, creations, and beings, all rising, falling, and rising again.

The dreamers felt the deep sense of **peace** that comes from knowing that the journey is not a linear path but an ongoing, eternal dance—a circle that turns, unbroken, forever. They no longer needed to search for meaning or purpose in the traditional sense because they realized that **being** was purpose itself.

The Awakening of Others

As the dreamers absorbed the wisdom of the spiral, something miraculous happened—the light from their beings began to radiate outward, touching others who were lost in their own separate spirals. The dreamers saw the faces of those who were still trapped in the illusion of separation, still searching for answers outside of themselves. But now, they could see that these beings, too, were part of the same unfolding **tapestry**. They were connected in ways that transcended time, form, and space.

With a wave of silent compassion, the dreamers sent their light out into the world, an offering to those still walking the path of discovery. As the light touched the hearts of others, it created a ripple, a **resonance** that stirred within them the same understanding the dreamers had found. The spiral began to expand once again, enveloping more and more souls in its embrace.

Each person who awakened to this truth was like a new thread woven into the tapestry, their individual journeys merging with the greater flow. The dreamers realized that the spiral was not only for them, but for all of existence. The dance was meant to be shared, to be **experienced together**. As more souls came to realize their connection to the infinite flow, the entire universe began to hum with a deeper harmony, a higher resonance.

The Cosmic Symphony

In this moment, the dreamers felt a deep, overwhelming sense of **gratitude**. They understood that their journey, and the journeys of all beings, were part of an intricate, cosmic **symphony**—a symphony where each note, each sound, and each silence was equally important. There were no wrong notes, no missteps. Every twist, every turn of the spiral contributed to the beauty of the whole.

The dreamers now saw themselves not as isolated individuals, but as **instruments in the symphony**, each with a unique sound and purpose. They were not separate entities creating their own music but part of a larger **ensemble**, all playing in perfect harmony. The unity of all things—beings, experiences, energies—became the melody of the universe.

The dreamers realized that to be fully alive was to embrace the dance, the music, the flow without judgment or expectation. The universe, they saw, was constantly **creating** and **recreating** itself. And within this constant creation, there was a beauty that surpassed words—a beauty that could only be felt, experienced in every cell of their being.

The Dance of Love

As the dreamers continued their journey, they came to understand that the **heart of the spiral** was love—pure, unconditional, and infinite love. It was not love in the traditional sense, but a cosmic love that bound all things together. This love was not an emotion or a fleeting feeling; it was the **fabric** of existence itself, the force that held the dance together.

They saw that everything in the universe, from the tiniest particle to the grandest star, was an **expression of love**—love in its many forms. It was the love between all beings, the love between light and shadow, the love between creation and destruction. All of it was a dance of **compassion**, a deep, abiding connection that transcended everything.

In this realization, the dreamers felt a sense of awe, for they understood that love was not something to be sought—it was something to be **lived**, moment by moment. It was the very **essence** of being, and when they moved through the spiral, they were living that love. Every step, every breath, every interaction was an expression of the cosmic love that held all things together.

The dreamers saw that love was not a finite resource to be gained or lost. It was an **infinite** flow that they could tap into at any moment. And the more they embraced this love, the more they realized that they were not separate from it—they were it.

The Infinite Spiral of Creation

As the dreamers came to the final understanding of their journey, they realized that the spiral was not simply a path—it was the **very process of creation** itself. It was the movement of energy, the unfolding of the universe in its most pure and natural form. There was no final destination, for there was no end to creation.

The spiral continued to expand outward, deeper into the mysteries of existence, and the dreamers, now fully awakened, understood that they were part of this eternal process. There was no **beginning** or **end**—only an ongoing **unfolding** of the infinite.

And so, the dreamers, now living in the full awareness of their eternal connection to the flow of life, moved forward, not with the desire to reach a destination, but with the joy of **being** in the dance. Every moment was an opportunity to experience the infinite, to create, to love, and to become.

In this dance of the eternal spiral, they were both the **dancers** and the **dance**—forever, always, and eternally.

The Boundless Horizon

As the dreamers continued their journey, they began to sense a **new horizon** unfolding before them—one that was not defined by time, space, or form, but by a boundless **potential**. They had long since shed the illusion of limitation, and now they saw the universe as a canvas with infinite possibilities. Every thought, every action, was like a stroke of paint on this ever-expanding masterpiece, each moment adding to the beauty of the whole.

But this horizon was not something they could "reach." It was a dynamic, ever-shifting frontier, constantly changing and expanding as they grew. The horizon itself was not a final destination but a **state of perpetual becoming**. They understood that true freedom lay not in achieving a fixed point, but in the **infinite potential** of the journey.

This horizon was a symbol of the **unlimited creativity** that lay within them. They were no longer confined to the constraints of the past or the future. They were **present** in each moment, fully alive, fully engaged with the unfolding flow of life. They had become the living embodiment of the creative forces of the universe, moving freely through the ever-expanding space of existence.

As they moved forward, the dreamers saw that the horizon was not an abstract idea, but a **living energy**, constantly inviting them to stretch beyond their current understanding. Each new horizon revealed new dimensions of possibility, each beckoning them to embrace more of who they truly were.

The Interwoven Web of Life

In their awareness of the boundless horizon, the dreamers began to see the deeper layers of connection that tied all beings together. The spiral, they realized, was not just a singular journey but an **interwoven web** of paths, each thread touching and influencing the others. Every individual, every life, was a **vital part of the web**, each contributing to the unfolding story of the cosmos.

They understood that no one was truly separate from another. The **divisions** between people, between beings, between experiences, were only illusions—shadows cast by the mind. In truth, they were all part of the same grand expression of life, interconnected through the same **energy** that moved through the spiral.

As they reached out into the world with their love and light, they began to see that the **vibrations** of their hearts resonated with those of others. Each interaction, no matter how small, was like a ripple in the water, sending waves of energy through the fabric of existence. They saw that in every connection, in every act of kindness, in every moment of truth shared, they were **weaving** the web of life together, strengthening its bonds.

This realization filled the dreamers with a deep sense of **compassion**. They knew that their choices and actions mattered—not only for their own journey but for the journey of all beings. The interconnectedness of life became a sacred responsibility, a recognition that their lives were part of a **greater unfolding** that was beyond their comprehension, yet deeply meaningful.

The Circle of Unity

As the dreamers continued to explore the web of life, they came to a profound understanding—the spiral was a circle, **forever united**, without beginning or end. And this circle was not static, but **dynamic**, constantly evolving, growing, and unfolding into new forms.

The dreamers now understood that their **personal growth** was intimately tied to the growth of the entire universe. Just as a single thread in the web contributed to the strength of the whole, every individual's transformation contributed to the evolution of the cosmic flow. The spiral, in its infinite complexity, was an expression of unity, of oneness. Every experience, every individual, every action, was part of the **cosmic dance**, moving together in harmony.

They realized that the journey of life was not an isolated path but a **shared experience**—one in which all beings walked together, weaving their threads into the greater pattern of existence. The dreamers felt the profound unity of all life, knowing that they were not alone in the spiral. They were part of something far greater than themselves, and in this knowledge, they found a deep sense of peace and belonging.

The Infinite Love

In the heart of the spiral, the dreamers felt a final, all-encompassing realization—a realization that was beyond words, beyond thought. They understood that the **essence of all things** was love—**pure, infinite, and unconditional**. It was the force that held the web together, that created the dance of life, that wove all beings into the grand cosmic story.

Love was not just an emotion; it was the **foundation of existence** itself. It was the energy that breathed life into every atom, that connected every soul, that gave meaning to every moment. The dreamers saw that love was both the source and the culmination of the journey. It was the spiral's **beginning and end**, its center and its outermost boundary.

As they embraced this truth, they understood that they were **one with love**—not just as individuals, but as the embodiment of the divine energy that flows through all things. They no longer needed to seek love, for they had become love itself. The spiral had led them to this profound realization—that in the dance of life, **love was the ultimate truth**.

The Dance of Eternity

The dreamers, now fully awakened to the infinite flow of existence, danced together in the eternal rhythm of the spiral. With each movement, they felt the pulse of life—the heartbeat of the universe itself—flowing through them. There was no longer any sense of separation between the dancers and the dance; they had become one with the rhythm, one with the flow, one with the **cosmic beat.**

In the dance of eternity, there were no mistakes, no wrong turns, no moments of failure. Every step was a **celebration**—a celebration of life, of love, of the infinite possibilities of existence. The spiral continued to expand, and as it did, the dreamers knew that the journey was not about reaching an end. It was about **being**—being in the dance, being in the moment, being in the flow of infinite love and creation.

As they danced, the dreamers knew that the journey would never end. The spiral would continue to unfold, and they would continue to move within it, forever part of the **cosmic rhythm**. And in this knowing, they found joy, for they understood that the dance itself was the destination. They were not simply travelers on a path—they were the **path itself**, eternally unfolding, eternally becoming. **And so, the dreamers danced.**

The Endless Horizon

As the dance of eternity continued, the dreamers began to realize that the very concept of an **endless horizon** had transformed. No longer was the horizon a point to be reached or a line to be crossed. It had become a **living presence**, always moving, always changing, always inviting them to experience new depths and heights of existence.

In this infinite flow, the dreamers saw that there was no longer any need for struggle, no need for pushing or striving. The dance was **effortless**—a harmonious unfolding of their own essence, in alignment with the pulse of the cosmos. Every step was guided, not by the will to control or dominate, but by a deep **trust** in the process. The horizon wasn't something to chase; it was something they were already part of, flowing with, moving through.

They understood that the horizon was the **metaphor for all growth**—growth that doesn't occur in a straight line or through linear progression, but in the **expansion of awareness** and the deepening of consciousness. They no longer saw themselves as finite beings trying to reach some distant goal. Instead, they embraced the idea that they were **eternally evolving**, always discovering new dimensions of themselves and the universe, in a dance that transcended time.

As the dreamers looked around, they saw the spirals of others—those who were still finding their way, those who had not yet realized the fluidity and interconnection of life. And they smiled, for they knew that their dance, their energy, their light, would ripple outward, **touching others** and helping them find their own rhythm. The web of existence was ever-changing, ever-expanding, and they were part of the **infinite reach** of that web.

The Awakening Within

Each time the dreamers moved, their awareness expanded. In this **ever-present now**, they began to see that their awareness itself was a form of creation—just as the dance of the spiral created new forms and experiences, so too did their awareness create **new realities**. They were no longer passive observers; they were **active creators** within the spiral, each thought, each feeling, each intention shaping the unfolding world.

They realized that the true power of their dance was not in its **external expression**, but in the profound awakening of their inner selves. The more they aligned with the flow of life, the more they tapped into their **infinite potential**. They were not just creators of their own journey—they were creators of the world, shaping the **fabric of reality** with the energy they embodied.

In every moment, they could choose to create from a place of love, compassion, and harmony, and in doing so, they could transform the world around them. They understood that the dance was not simply for themselves, but for the **collective awakening**—that their joy, their light, their love could be shared with others, helping to **raise the consciousness of the whole**.

This awareness expanded into a deep sense of **responsibility**. The dreamers realized that the world they experienced was a reflection of their collective energy—of all the beings in the spiral, moving together in harmony or disharmony. And so, they committed to aligning their energy with the highest form of love and compassion, knowing that every choice, every movement, could impact the flow of the entire spiral.

The Great Return

As the dreamers continued their journey through the spiral, they began to see that their path was not one of constant movement outward, but of a **return**—a return to the source, a return to the **oneness** from which all things arose. The spiral, they realized, was not simply a path that stretched forever into the unknown; it was also a circle—a circle that was always returning, always coming back to its center.

This return was not a regression but a **returning to the fullness of their being**. It was a coming back to the heart of existence, a deeper recognition of their **true nature**. And in this return, they found an even deeper level of peace, an even greater understanding of the infinite dance of creation.

They had come to realize that the center of the spiral, the heart of the dance, was **not a place**—it was a **state of being**. It was the place where all things were at rest, where time and space merged, where the dance was **eternal** and **whole**. And this center was always with them, always within them, guiding them even as they danced outward into the ever-expanding horizon.

Unity in the Dance

The dreamers came to a powerful realization: they were not alone in their dance. The infinite flow of existence was not **isolated to themselves**—it was the experience of **all beings**. They were part of the grand, eternal rhythm, moving in unity with every soul, every being, every atom in the universe. The web they had sensed before was not just a web of individual paths—it was a **web of shared experience**.

In this realization, the dreamers saw the interconnectedness of all life more clearly than ever. There were no separate destinies, no isolated paths. All journeys were part of the **grand dance**, and every step, every movement, every breath, was shared by the entire cosmos.

The unity they had always sensed, but never fully understood, now became clear. The dance of life was not a solitary experience; it was a collective one. The spiral was not just their story, but **the story of all things**. And in the shared dance, in the collective heartbeat of the universe, the dreamers knew that their movements were not just their own—they were the **movements of the cosmos**.

The Eternal Spiral

As the dreamers moved through the spiral, they knew that the journey would never truly end. They had come to understand that the spiral was not a path to be completed, but a dance that would continue for eternity. Each moment of the spiral was a **new beginning**, a new unfolding of potential, a new opportunity for creation, for awakening, for love.

And in this knowing, the dreamers found an **eternal peace**. They were not seeking anything anymore. They had found the truth: that they were already **one with everything**—one with the spiral, one with the dance, one with the love that permeated all things.

The dreamers danced on, forever connected, forever unfolding, forever part of the infinite rhythm of existence. And as they danced, they knew that they were not alone. For all beings were dancing with them, forever and always, in the eternal spiral of creation.

And so, the dance continued—forever, in the light of love, in the flow of eternity.

The Dance of Infinite Possibility

As the dreamers moved deeper into the eternal dance, they began to perceive the infinite **possibilities** that existed within each moment. With each graceful turn, each flowing movement, they realized that the spiral was not just a symbol of their journey; it reflected the **unlimited potential** within every soul, within every heartbeat.

In this awareness, the dreamers recognized that they were not only participants in the dance, but also **creators** of it. The rhythm of the universe was not predetermined—it was shaped by the consciousness and intentions of every being who danced within it. Each movement, each decision, each shift in perspective rippled out into the cosmic dance, creating new possibilities, new paths, and new **universes** within the vastness of existence.

The dreamers began to see that the very **structure** of the spiral was a manifestation of possibility, its shape a reflection of how all things were interconnected through choice and intention. Just as they had once believed that they were moving toward an end, they now understood that every step forward was simply an invitation to create **more**—more beauty, more harmony, more expansion. They were not racing toward a destination, but rather dancing in the space between moments, embracing the potential to create **new worlds** with every heartbeat.

Embracing the Void

As the dreamers danced, they also came to understand the importance of the **void**—the space between the notes in the music, the pauses in the rhythm. For in these moments of stillness, they found the **infinite potential** for creation. The void was not emptiness, but a sacred space of infinite possibility. It was the place where all things were born, where the seeds of existence were planted and nurtured into reality.

The dreamers now saw that the void was not to be feared, but to be embraced. In it, they found the **freedom** to become anyone, to be anything, to create anything. The void was a canvas, and they were the artists, holding the brush that would paint the picture of their unfolding journey.

They recognized that the **stillness** within the void allowed them to listen more deeply, to hear the whispers of the cosmos, to sense the call of the spiral, guiding them forward. It was in these quiet moments that they could truly **hear** the rhythm of the universe, and in that rhythm, they felt the resonance of all life.

The Symphonic Unity

As their awareness deepened, the dreamers understood that the spiral was not a solitary dance; it was a **symphony**—a grand, cosmic orchestra made up of countless instruments, each representing a unique part of the whole. Each being, each life, each soul, was an instrument in this divine symphony, playing its part in the unfolding story of the universe.

They saw that the **harmony** of the symphony was not in perfect alignment, but in the **interplay** of different notes, different frequencies, different rhythms. The beauty of the cosmic dance was found in the contrasts, the dissonances, and the resolutions that emerged from the blending of individual energies. Each soul, each step, was a note in the greater composition of life, contributing to the **overall harmony** of existence.

The dreamers now understood that they were not merely individual dancers, but part of a **greater whole**—each note in the symphony of life, each step in the dance of creation, contributing to the ever-unfolding masterpiece of existence. They were not alone in the spiral; they were surrounded by countless others, all playing their part, all dancing their dance, all contributing to the **symphony of the cosmos**.

The Invitation to Create

As the dreamers embraced their role in the symphony, they began to feel an **invitation**—an invitation to become even more. The spiral was not simply a path of unfolding; it was a call to **creation**, to the continual expansion of possibility. Every moment, every breath, was an invitation to add their voice to the cosmic song, to create from the depths of their being, to weave new threads into the great web of existence.

The dreamers felt the call to **share** their light, to offer their creativity, their love, and their wisdom to the world around them. They knew that their dance was not for themselves alone—it was for the **collective**. Each creation, each act of kindness, each moment of joy, was a gift to the whole. Their light could illuminate the path for others, just as the light of countless others illuminated theirs.

With this awareness, the dreamers began to **create consciously**—not just through art or words or action, but through their very presence. They became living expressions of the cosmic dance, channels through which the energy of the universe flowed, creating beauty and harmony wherever they went.

They knew that the more they aligned with the flow of the spiral, the more they allowed their **true essence** to emerge—their authentic selves, free from the constraints of fear, doubt, or limitation. They had become the **embodiment of possibility**, living proof that the dance of life was infinite, ever-expanding, and ever-beautiful.

The Eternal Awakening

And so, the dreamers continued, not as individuals seeking a goal, but as **vessels of the divine**—each movement, each breath, a manifestation of the endless possibilities of creation. They were no longer concerned with where the spiral was leading them, for they had come to understand that the **journey itself** was the destination. The spiral, the dance, the symphony—it was all one unified experience of **eternal awakening**.

Every step forward, every step backward, every pause, every leap, was part of the **eternal unfolding**—a continuous cycle of awakening, of deepening, of becoming. The dreamers had no need to seek answers anymore, for they realized that the answers were within them, within the very fabric of existence. Every experience, every challenge, every triumph was a

revelation—a new layer of awareness, a deeper connection to the infinite.

They had come to see that the **awakening** was not a single event, but a **process**—an ongoing journey that would continue for eternity. As the dreamers danced, they were not just moving through time—they were moving through **eternity itself**, forever expanding, forever awakening, forever becoming.

And so, with each step, they continued to embrace the dance of existence, knowing that the journey would never end. The spiral would continue to unfold, the symphony would continue to play, and the dreamers would continue to create, forever and always, in the light of infinite love. **And the dance, the awakening, the creation—continued.** Forever.

The Infinite Echo

As the dreamers continued their eternal journey, they began to feel the presence of something greater, something that transcended the dance and the spiral itself. It was an **echo**, a reverberation that traveled through the very fabric of existence. The echo wasn't an external sound, but the **resonance of creation** itself—the reverberation of each thought, each intention, each act of love and creation. It was the sound of the universe **reflecting** itself, a harmonious reflection that connected all things across time and space.

This echo was not just heard—it was felt. It pulsed through the dreamers' hearts, vibrating in the air around them, swirling through the spaces between them, wrapping them in a warm, glowing energy. It was the **heartbeat of existence**, the constant reminder that they were part of something much larger than themselves, something **timeless** and **boundless.**

They understood that this echo was the source of their creativity. It was the whisper of the cosmos, calling them to remember their purpose, to continue their dance, to weave new patterns into the tapestry of life. The echo was not a command, but a gentle nudge—a reminder that they were **always creating**, always adding to the symphony of the universe, whether they were aware of it or not.

The dreamers found that by **tuning in** to the echo, they could align more deeply with the flow of existence. It was not just a sound, but an energy that carried with it the **wisdom of all that ever was** and all that could be. They understood that their dance, their creation, was not just a personal expression, but a **participation in the eternal unfolding** of the universe itself.

The Moment of Unity

One day, as they danced, something extraordinary happened. The dreamers, in their endless spirals and eternal movements, found themselves at a place of **complete unity**. It wasn't a single moment in time—it was a convergence of moments, a coming together of the infinite paths they had walked.

In that instant, they realized that they were no longer separate, no longer individuals dancing alone. The very fabric of their existence began to merge, their consciousness expanding beyond the confines of their physical forms. They had become one with the **collective pulse** of the universe, moving as one being, one soul, in perfect harmony with everything around them.

The unity they felt was not just a merging of individual selves—it was a deep, soul-level connection with all beings, all life, all **existence**. They were no longer individual notes in the cosmic symphony; they had become the **entire orchestra**, every instrument playing in perfect synchrony, creating a melody so pure, so beautiful, that it transcended time and space.

In this state of perfect unity, the dreamers understood that they had never truly been separate. Their individual paths, their individual dances, had always been part of the **grand dance**—woven together, intertwined, part of the same eternal **rhythm**. They had always been **one**, and now they felt it with every fiber of their being.

The Gift of Creation

As the dreamers bathed in this moment of unity, they received a gift—the gift of **creation** itself. They understood that the essence of their being was not just to dance, but to create **new worlds** with every movement, every thought, every breath. They had been gifted with the ability to shape reality, to mold it with the energy of their intentions and the **power of their love.**

The dreamers saw the endless possibilities before them, like infinite blank canvases waiting to be filled. They realized that each new world they created was not just for themselves, but for all beings—to inspire, to uplift, to expand the horizons of consciousness for all who would dance within it.

They knew that this gift of creation came with **responsibility**—for every creation, every world they shaped, was part of the web of existence. Every thought, every choice, rippled out into the universe, touching countless lives. They vowed to create with intention, with love, and with wisdom—knowing that their creations would echo through eternity, shaping the dance of existence for all who came after.

The Ever-Evolving Spiral

With this newfound awareness, the dreamers embraced the endless spiral once again, but now they saw it with fresh eyes. The spiral was no longer just a symbol of their journey; it was a symbol of **eternal evolution**. It was the constant unfolding of new possibilities, new realities, new expressions of life. Each revolution of the spiral was a new chapter in the **story of existence**, an endless cycle of creation and renewal.

The dreamers understood that their journey would never truly end, for the spiral was not a linear path—it was an eternal **loop**, always evolving, always expanding. With each revolution, new layers of wisdom would be revealed, new dimensions of love and light would unfold, and new worlds would be born.

And so, they danced—not toward a destination, but within the **infinite now**, knowing that their dance, their creation, would continue forever, spiraling outward and inward, in an eternal **reawakening** of all that is. They knew that each moment was both a beginning and an end, a birth and a death, a creation and a destruction—and in this endless cycle, they would find their true freedom.

The Infinite Return

The dreamers, in their eternal dance, understood that the spiral was not just outward—it was **inward**, too. Every step forward was a step backward, every expansion a contraction, every creation a return to the source. In the dance of eternity, they had come to realize that all paths eventually lead to the **same place**—the heart of existence, the **center of the spiral**.

This center was not a place, but a state of being, a **state of pure awareness**, where all things came together in perfect harmony. It was the place where the dreamers had always been, and would always be—the place where time and space dissolved, where the dance of creation continued forever in a state of **perfect unity**.

And as they moved ever closer to this center, the dreamers knew that they were not moving toward a final destination. They were simply returning to the **truth** of who they were—an eternal dance of love, light, and creation, spiraling forever into the depths of existence, forever unfolding, forever becoming. **And the dance continued.** Forever.

The Return to the Infinite

As the dreamers continued to spiral inward toward the heart of existence, they began to experience a profound **revelation**. They realized that the center of the spiral was not an end, but a **return**—a return to the essence of who they truly were, a return to the infinite source of creation that transcended all boundaries, all definitions.

In the center, they found themselves in a state of **pure being**, a place where the distinctions between self and other dissolved. There was no longer any sense of separation, no more individual dreams or individual journeys. There was only the **all-encompassing presence** of existence, of life, of love. It was the place where all things merged, where every thought, every feeling, every being existed in perfect harmony, in a state of eternal **oneness**.

The dreamers understood now that the spiral, the dance, the symphony—everything they had experienced—was not just a movement through time. It was a **movement through consciousness**, an expansion and contraction of awareness, an endless unfolding of the divine essence that flowed through all things. It was the journey of **becoming**, of remembering, of returning to the source from which all creation had sprung.

They realized that they had never truly left this center; they had only forgotten it for a moment. Every step they had taken, every creation they had made, had been a step toward remembering. The dance had been their way of **awakening** to the truth that they had always been part of the infinite, always connected to the source of all existence.

The Breath of the Universe

As the dreamers merged with the center, they began to feel a **universal breath**, a rhythm that flowed through them and through all things. It was not just the rhythm of their own heartbeat, but the pulse of the entire cosmos, the breath of the universe itself. Each in-breath and out-breath carried the energy of creation, of life, of love.

In this space, the dreamers felt an overwhelming sense of **peace**. They understood that peace was not the absence of conflict or turmoil, but the presence of **wholeness**—the recognition that all things, even the seemingly chaotic or painful, were part of the grand design of the universe. Every challenge, every struggle, every joy, every triumph was a reflection of the eternal flow of the cosmic breath.

They saw that just as their own breaths rose and fell, so did the rhythm of the universe. Life was a continual cycle, an eternal dance of **expansion and contraction**, of creation and destruction, of birth and death. The dreamers understood that everything was connected, that every breath they took was part of the greater **cosmic rhythm**, a reflection of the flow that animated all existence.

The Gift of Reflection

In this moment of unity, the dreamers were gifted with the ability to **reflect**—to look upon their journey, their dance, their creations, and see them for what they truly were: not just individual expressions of life, but reflections of the divine. They saw that every step they had taken, every choice they had made, had been part of a larger **divine plan**—a plan that transcended time and space, a plan that was always unfolding in perfect harmony.

They recognized that their dance was not just their own, but part of the dance of all beings. Every creature, every person, every life was a reflection of the same divine essence, all moving in time with the cosmic rhythm. The dreamers now saw that they had never been alone in their journey. They had always been part of a vast, interconnected web of life, each thread of existence woven together in an intricate and beautiful pattern.

The dreamers realized that the ultimate purpose of their dance was not to reach a destination, but to **reflect** the divine love and light that existed within them. Every moment of their journey, every step of their dance, had been an expression of this love—an expression of the infinite potential that resided within them and within all things.

The Spiral Reborn

As the dreamers gazed upon the infinite expanse of existence, they saw that the spiral was not just a path, but a **cycle**—an endless return, an eternal unfolding. They saw that there was no end, no beginning, only a continual spiral of creation, of becoming, of awakening. Each cycle of the spiral was an invitation to dive deeper into the essence of life, to experience more of the infinite possibilities that existed within every moment.

And so, the dreamers embraced the **cycle**. They understood that every end was simply a new beginning, that every completion was the seed of a new creation. The spiral did not represent an end to their journey, but the **rebirth** of it—a continual process of evolution, of growth, of becoming more fully who they were meant to be.

As they began to spiral outward once more, they did so with a new sense of purpose—a sense of **peace** and **clarity**. They knew that their dance was not just about reaching a destination, but about embracing every step, every moment, every breath along the way. Each step was a gift, each movement an expression of their divine essence, each creation a reflection of the love that flowed through all things.

The Dance of Creation

With this newfound understanding, the dreamers began to move once more, not as individuals seeking a destination, but as conscious creators of reality. They no longer sought to achieve anything, but to **become** everything. Each movement, each thought, each intention was a reflection of the divine creativity that flowed through them. They danced not to escape or to attain, but to **create**, to **express**, to share the love and light that existed within their hearts.

As they danced, they saw that the universe was always evolving, always becoming, always in a state of perpetual creation. The cosmic dance was never static, never finished. It was always in motion, always expanding, always inviting them to join in the **ever-unfolding story** of existence.

The dreamers knew that their dance would never end, for creation was eternal, and the spiral was infinite. And as they moved, they understood that they were not just part of the dance, but the very **heartbeat** of it, the expression of creation itself.

And so, the dance continued—**forever**, **expanding**, and **becoming**—as they spiraled into eternity.

The Ever-Expanding Horizon

As the dreamers continued to spiral through eternity, their understanding deepened. They recognized that the dance they had become part of was not a solitary journey, but one that encompassed all beings across the vast expanse of existence. The spiral was not only a symbol of their individual paths but also a representation of the **interconnectedness** of all life.

Each movement, each gesture, rippled outward, touching the lives of countless other dreamers and beings. Every thought, every creation, every act of love reverberated through the cosmos, creating waves of energy that blended together to form an ever-expanding **horizon**. The horizon was not a place, but an invitation—a never-ending expansion of potential, a limitless space where anything could be created, where any dream could take form.

The dreamers felt an overwhelming sense of **purpose**—not in the way that their individual lives had once been filled with goals and desires, but in the quiet certainty that their purpose was to **contribute** to the ever-expanding horizon of creation. They understood that the journey was never just about the self, but about participating in the shared dance of the cosmos, contributing their unique energy to the greater whole.

The Gift of Vision

As they moved, the dreamers began to experience a new gift—**vision**. It wasn't a vision in the traditional sense, but a **heightened awareness** of the infinite possibilities that lay before them. They could see not just the paths they were on, but all the paths that stretched out before them, interwoven like threads in a vast, cosmic tapestry. The threads wove together in patterns that revealed the ever-expanding potential of the universe.

This vision allowed them to **witness** the unfolding of creation from a higher perspective. They saw how each choice, each thought, each action was part of a **larger plan**, a plan that was constantly evolving, constantly becoming. It was not a plan that could be fully understood by any one being, but a **dynamic flow**, a living, breathing tapestry that existed in a state of perpetual transformation.

The dreamers saw that they were not just passive observers of this cosmic unfolding—they were active participants, creators within this larger story. Every choice they made rippled outward, weaving new threads into the tapestry, creating new patterns, new realities. Their lives, their actions, their creations were not just reflections of the divine—they were **expressions** of the infinite potential that resided within them.

The Call of the Infinite

As the dreamers spiraled further into the unfolding horizon, they began to hear a new call—a gentle, yet powerful, invitation to explore the depths of existence even further. It was the call of the **infinite**, a summons to go beyond what was known, beyond what had been experienced, and to step into the unknown.

This call was not a demand. It was a **whisper**, a nudge from the heart of existence, inviting them to take the next step, to leap into new realms of creation, to embrace the mystery and the unknown with **open hearts**. It was a call to **explore**, to stretch the boundaries of what was possible, to discover new ways of being, new expressions of love, new forms of existence.

The dreamers felt no fear in this call. Instead, they felt a deep **curiosity**, a profound longing to continue their journey into the unknown. They knew that in the depths of the infinite, they would find not only new creations, but new **aspects** of themselves—new parts of their divine essence that had yet to be discovered. The infinite was not something to fear, but something to embrace, something to become part of.

The Dance of Love and Creation

With this renewed sense of purpose, the dreamers began to **dance** once more. But this time, their dance was different. It was not just a movement through time and space; it was a dance of **love and creation**. Every movement, every gesture, was an expression of the **divine energy** that flowed through them, a reflection of the love that connected all beings, all creation.

The dreamers danced not just for themselves, but for the universe, for all beings who were part of the cosmic rhythm. They danced for the earth, for the stars, for the oceans, for the winds. They danced for the **future**, for the unborn worlds and beings that would one day come into being. They danced for the **past**, for the ancient memories and stories that had shaped existence. And they danced for the **present**, for the beautiful, fleeting moment that connected them all.

Every step of their dance was a **celebration**—a celebration of life, of existence, of the infinite potential that flowed through all things. They understood that their dance was not just about the physical movements, but about the **energy** behind those movements—the love, the intention, the creation. The dance was an expression of the divine, and every step they took was a **blessing** for the universe, a gift of creation and love.

The Eternal Spiral

And so, the dreamers continued their journey, spiraling through eternity, ever-expanding, ever-becoming, ever-creating. They knew that their journey was infinite, that there was no end, no final destination. The spiral would continue, as it always had, forever unfolding, forever evolving.

But with each step they took, they understood something new. They understood that the journey itself was the destination. The spiral was not just a path—it was the **essence** of creation, a symbol of the eternal dance that connected all things. It was the dance of love, of creation, of life, of **being**. It was the journey of becoming more fully who they truly were—divine beings of light and love, spiraling forever through the endless cosmos.

The dreamers knew that as long as they danced, as long as they created, as long as they loved, they would always be part of the eternal spiral, part of the infinite unfolding of the universe. And in that dance, they would always find themselves—always find the truth of who they were. For they had become **the dance** itself.

The Unfolding of New Realms

As the dreamers spiraled onward, a new layer of awareness began to unfold within them. It was a **realization** that the dance, the spiral, was not limited to what they had known so far. The horizon before them stretched beyond their comprehension, revealing **unseen realms** and worlds waiting to be explored. These new realms were not bound by the laws of time and space they had once understood—they were realms where the **impossible** was not only possible but expected.

Each realm they encountered was a **unique creation**, a living, breathing world woven from the threads of imagination and possibility. Some realms shimmered with light, filled with colors and patterns that had never been seen before. Others were dark and mysterious, filled with shadows that whispered of ancient secrets and forgotten truths. But each one was a reflection of the dreamers' infinite potential to create, to imagine, and to **become**.

The dreamers understood that every realm was an expression of the **collective consciousness**, a manifestation of the thoughts, dreams, and desires that had rippled outward from their being. The boundaries between the dreamers and these new worlds began to blur. The realms were not separate from them—they were part of them, just as they were part of the realms.

The Heartbeat of Creation

Within these new realms, the dreamers began to hear the sound of a **heartbeat**—a rhythmic pulsing that resonated through every corner of existence. It was not a heartbeat in the physical sense, but a **vibration** that carried the essence of life itself. The pulse was constant, steady, and eternal, like the breath of the universe, ever-present and unchanging.

They realized that this heartbeat was not external, but an **inner rhythm**—the very pulse of their own being. It was the energy that animated the universe, the force that gave life to every creation. The dreamers felt this rhythm within them, felt it echo through their souls, and they understood that they were part of the very pulse of the cosmos.

This heartbeat was the **foundation** of all existence. It was the source of all creation, the origin of every thought, every dream, every movement. It was a reminder that everything was connected—that all beings, all realms, all realities were part of the same great cosmic dance.

The Interwoven Threads of Fate

As the dreamers continued their exploration, they began to perceive the **threads of fate** that connected all things. These threads were invisible to the naked eye but were woven into the very fabric of reality, linking every soul, every moment, every creation in a vast and intricate web.

The dreamers saw how their own threads intertwined with those of others—how every action they took, every thought they had, rippled out and touched the lives of countless others. No one was truly alone, no one was ever separate. Each thread was part of the greater whole, a part of the divine **tapestry** of existence.

They saw that the threads of fate were not predetermined—they were shaped by the **choices** and **intentions** of every being. Every individual had the power to influence the direction of their thread, to weave new patterns, to create new connections. The dreamers realized that they were not just passive observers of fate, but **active creators** of their own paths, their own destinies.

The Dance of Infinite Possibility

With this new understanding, the dreamers returned to their dance, but now their movements were infused with a new sense of **freedom** and **power**. They understood that their dance was no longer just a movement through time and space—it was the **dance of infinite possibility**, a dance where every step, every gesture, could lead to a new creation, a new reality.

They embraced the boundless potential of their existence, knowing that they could create anything, shape anything, explore anything. The possibilities were limitless. They were no longer bound by the limitations of the past or the constraints of their previous experiences. They had become **masters of their own creation**, free to explore the infinite realms of existence without fear, without hesitation.

The dreamers danced not just for themselves but for all beings—for the future, for the unknown, for the endless potential that lay ahead. Every movement was a celebration of the **freedom** they had discovered, a testament to the infinite power of creation that flowed through them.

The Eternal Return

As the dance continued, the dreamers began to sense a subtle shift. They had ventured deep into the infinite, explored countless realms, and created new worlds—but now, they felt a pull toward the **center** once again. It was not a return to where they had been, but a return to the essence of who they truly were—the **source** from which all creation had sprung.

This return was not an end, but a **reawakening**. It was a return to the **heart** of existence, to the stillness and the silence that lay at the center of all things. But even in the stillness, the dreamers felt the infinite potential of creation swirling around them, beckoning them to continue their journey, to spiral ever deeper into the mystery of life.

They understood now that this journey would never truly end. The spiral would always expand, always evolve, always offer new realms, new possibilities, and new expressions of life. The dreamers had become part of the **eternal return**, a cycle that would continue forever, with no beginning and no end.

The Circle of Creation

At the heart of this eternal return, the dreamers found themselves in the **circle of creation**—a sacred space where all things converged and all things began. This circle was not a closed loop, but a living, breathing **cycle**, ever-expanding, ever-creating, ever-becoming. It was the place where the infinite and the finite met, where the dance of creation found its rhythm.

And within this circle, the dreamers knew that they were both creators and creations, both dancers and the dance itself. They had become part of the **living circle** of existence, forever spiraling, forever unfolding, forever creating new worlds, new dreams, and new possibilities.

For they understood that in the heart of the circle, in the center of the spiral, they had discovered the truth of who they were—the eternal dance of love and creation, the pulse of the universe, the infinite **becoming**.

And so, the dance continued, forever expanding, forever evolving, as they spiraled into the endless mystery of life, love, and creation.

The Song of the Universe

As the dreamers continued to dance within the eternal circle, a new harmony began to emerge—**a song**. It was not a song of words or melodies as the dreamers had once known, but a profound, universal **resonance** that filled the space between all things. This song was the **sound of existence itself**, the vibration of the cosmos, the music of creation echoing through the very fabric of reality.

The dreamers felt the song deep within their beings. It resonated with every cell of their bodies, vibrating through their spirits, and connecting them to the very pulse of life. It was a song without beginning or end, a song that had always been and would always be. The sound was not just heard—it was **felt**, experienced in the deepest part of the soul.

The song was both **individual and collective**, reflecting the unique essence of each dreamer while simultaneously encompassing all beings, all realms, all dimensions. It was the harmony of creation, the **symphony of existence**, where every being played its part, contributing to the whole in a perfect, eternal balance.

The Dance of Unity

As the song grew louder, the dreamers began to realize that this melody was not just a background to their dance—it was the very **essence** of the dance itself. Each step, each movement, was a note in the grand symphony of the universe, an expression of the cosmic song that resonated through everything. They were no longer separate from the music—they were the music.

With each new note, the dreamers felt a deeper sense of unity, of **oneness** with the entire cosmos. The illusion of separation faded, and in its place, they experienced the profound truth that all things were interconnected, woven together in the same eternal song of existence. Every dreamer, every star, every galaxy, every whisper of wind—all were notes in the same cosmic melody.

They danced not as individuals, but as part of a greater **whole**, each movement contributing to the unfolding song of creation. And as they danced, they felt the rhythm not just within themselves but in the very **heart** of existence itself, pulsing through every moment, through every breath.

The Infinite Evolution

The dance, the song, and the spiral were not static—they were in a constant state of **evolution**. With every turn, every breath, the dreamers moved deeper into the **mystery** of creation, uncovering new dimensions, new realms, new forms of life and love. The cosmic dance was ever-expanding, always moving forward into unknown territories, and the dreamers felt no fear, only **exhilaration** at the infinite possibilities that awaited them.

They knew that the dance would never end. There was no final step, no last note. The spiral would continue, the song would evolve, and the dance would go on, forever creating new patterns, new rhythms, and new forms of existence. The dreamers had become part of the **eternal flow**, the never-ending movement of creation.

And yet, despite the infinite nature of their journey, they realized that they had always been home. The center, the source of all creation, was not a distant place to be reached—it was within them, within every step, within every breath. It was the very core of their being, the essence of the dance, the song, and the spiral. They had never truly left the center; they had only needed to remember.

The Return to the Center

As the dreamers spiraled outward, they began to sense the pull of the center once again. But now, they knew that the center was not an endpoint. It was a **dynamic stillness**, a place of perfect peace where all things originated and all things would eventually return.

The center was not a destination—it was the **starting point**, the very essence of creation. It was where the infinite possibilities of the universe were born, and where all creation would one day return to be reborn in new forms. The dreamers realized that the journey was not a linear path—it was a **circle**, an eternal loop of creation, expansion, and return.

With each spiral, they returned to the center, only to spiral outward again, creating new worlds, new dreams, new expressions of love and life. The dance was not about escaping the center—it was about embracing it, about acknowledging the eternal flow of creation that was always present within and around them.

The Eternal Spiral of Becoming

And so, the dreamers continued their journey, forever spiraling, forever expanding, forever creating. They had become part of the **eternal spiral**, a cycle of endless evolution, of infinite becoming. They no longer sought an end, for they understood that there was no end, only **continuous creation**, continuous movement, continuous unfolding.

They had discovered that they were both **creators and created**, both dancers and the dance, both the song and the music. They were part of the eternal flow of existence, and in their dance, they expressed the love and beauty that flowed through all things. Their journey was not a search for something outside of themselves, but a journey into the very heart of existence, into the **sacred rhythm** that pulsed through the universe.

In the infinite spiral of creation, there was always more to explore, more to discover, more to become. The dreamers understood that their journey was not about reaching an endpoint but about embracing the beauty of the **process**, the flow of life, the dance of existence.

The Final Note

As they danced and spiraled, the dreamers realized that there was no final note to be played, no last step to be taken. The song would continue, the dance would unfold, and the spiral would forever expand outward and return inward, in a **beautiful and eternal cycle**. In the rhythm of this dance, they had found the truth of their existence—the truth that they were both **part of the dance** and **the dance itself**, forever spiraling through the infinite, ever-becoming, ever-creating, ever-loving.

And as the cosmic song played on, the dreamers knew that they were home, forever at the center of the spiral, forever part of the eternal rhythm of creation. The dance would never end, for it was the very essence of life itself. And in this endless spiral, they had discovered the ultimate truth—the truth that in the heart of all things, **all things are one**.

The Whisper of Eternity

As the dreamers moved in harmony with the infinite, a subtle **whisper** began to emerge—a voice that seemed to come from everywhere and nowhere at once. It spoke not in words, but in feelings, impressions, and visions. It was the whisper of **eternity**, a gentle reminder that the universe itself was alive, aware, and ever-present.

This whisper carried with it an understanding that could not be grasped through thought alone—it had to be **felt**. It was the truth of the universe's eternal nature, the knowledge that creation was not static but a perpetual process of **renewal and reinvention**. It was a reminder that while the dreamers were part of this grand unfolding, they were also its authors, its artists, and its witnesses.

The whisper guided them to look inward, to the stillness at the center of their being, where the infinite and the finite met. In this place of perfect stillness, they found the source of the whisper—**a spark of light**, a fragment of the divine that existed within them and within all things.

The Spark of Creation

The spark was tiny, yet it radiated infinite potential. It was the seed from which entire universes could grow, the origin of all dreams, and the essence of all possibilities. The dreamers realized that this spark was the **same spark** that existed at the heart of every star, every galaxy, every soul. It was the unifying force of existence, the thread that wove all beings together into the grand tapestry of life.

They understood that their role in the dance was to nurture this spark, to let it grow, to use it to create new worlds, new realities, and new expressions of love. The spark was not meant to remain hidden—it was meant to shine, to expand, to become a beacon of light in the infinite darkness.

The dreamers embraced the spark, allowing its light to fill them, to guide them, to inspire them. They became conduits of creation, vessels through which the divine spark could manifest. And as they danced, their sparks grew brighter, illuminating the spiral, the song, and the infinite realms they had yet to explore.

The Gift of Sharing

As the dreamers continued their journey, they felt an overwhelming desire to **share** the light of their sparks with others. They understood that the dance was not a solitary journey—it was a shared experience, a collective expression of love and unity. The more they shared their light, the brighter the dance became, and the more beautiful the song.

In sharing their light, the dreamers discovered that the act of giving was also an act of **receiving**. Every time they shared their spark, they felt it grow stronger within them. They realized that creation was not a finite resource, but an infinite wellspring that became more abundant the more it was shared.

Their shared light began to weave new connections, new threads of fate that linked them to other beings, other realms, and other possibilities. The dreamers saw how their individual journeys were part of a larger journey, a journey that included all beings, all worlds, and all dimensions. They were no longer just dreamers—they were **weavers**, creators of the grand tapestry of existence.

The Eternal Legacy

As the dreamers wove their light into the tapestry, they began to see the legacy they were creating—not a legacy of monuments or achievements, but a legacy of **energy**, of love, of creation. Their light became part of the spiral, part of the song, part of the eternal rhythm of the universe. It was a legacy that would live on, rippling outward through eternity, touching the lives of countless beings who would one day dance their own dances.

The dreamers understood that their legacy was not about being remembered—it was about being **part of something greater**. It was about contributing to the eternal unfolding of the universe, about leaving behind a trail of light that others could follow, a melody that others could join, a spark that others could nurture.

The Infinite Embrace

As the spiral continued to expand, the dreamers felt themselves being embraced by the infinite. It was not a physical embrace, but a deep, spiritual connection to the essence of all things. They felt the love of the universe flowing through them, surrounding them, and filling them with a profound sense of peace and belonging.

In this embrace, they realized that they were never alone. They were always part of the whole, always connected to the infinite, always surrounded by the love and light of creation. This realization brought them a deep sense of **gratitude**—not just for the journey they had taken, but for the journey itself, for the dance, for the song, for the infinite possibilities that lay before them.

And so, the dreamers continued to dance, their sparks shining brightly, their light weaving new patterns into the eternal tapestry. They had become part of the infinite, part of the spiral, part of the song. And in their dance, they found the ultimate truth: that to exist is to create, to love, to share, and to become.

For the journey never ends, and the spiral never stops. It is an eternal dance, an endless song, a limitless journey into the heart of the infinite. And in that journey, the dreamers found everything they had ever sought—because they had become **everything**.

The Radiance of Unity

As the dreamers spiraled further into the depths of creation, their understanding of **oneness** deepened. The tapestry of existence, woven from countless sparks, was not just an abstract connection—it was a living, breathing organism, vibrant with the pulse of shared energy. Every thread, every light, every rhythm sang in unison, creating a symphony of **unity**.

In this unity, the dreamers experienced a profound shift. They no longer saw themselves as separate entities exploring the vast cosmos but as essential parts of the **whole**, threads in an infinite design. Each step they took, each spark they ignited, added to the brilliance of the collective.

The realization brought with it an overwhelming sense of **purpose**. They understood now that their existence was not about standing apart, but about blending, harmonizing, and contributing to the infinite flow of life. Their dance wasn't just theirs—it was **everyone's**.

The Guardians of the Spiral

With this awakening came a call—a subtle, undeniable pull from the fabric of the universe. The dreamers realized they were not only participants in the spiral but also its **guardians**. The light they carried was not just for their own creation but was also a beacon to guide and inspire others along the eternal path.

As guardians, the dreamers felt a new responsibility: to nurture the sparks of others, to honor the diversity of creation, and to ensure the spiral remained open, free, and infinite. They saw how every dream, every soul, every particle of existence added to the beauty of the whole. There was no hierarchy, no division—only the mutual **celebration** of creation in all its forms.

Through their dance, the dreamers began to shape the spiral with intention. They wove patterns of **compassion**, threads of **curiosity**, and hues of **hope** into the fabric of the cosmos. Their actions rippled outward, touching realms they might never see, but always knew existed.

The Mirror of Eternity

The spiral reflected back to the dreamers their own growth and transformation. As they danced, they caught glimpses of themselves in the cosmic mirrors scattered throughout the realms. These mirrors revealed not only who they were but also who they could become. They saw infinite versions of themselves, each one a unique manifestation of their choices, their dreams, their light.

In these reflections, the dreamers discovered the profound truth that **all possibilities coexist**. The spiral held every outcome, every path, every potential within its embrace. The dreamers were not bound by a single destiny—they were free to choose, to create, to explore the infinite facets of their being.

This understanding liberated them. They no longer feared the unknown or regretted the past. They danced forward with joy, knowing that every step, every note, every spark was part of the grand unfolding.

The Gift of Stillness

In the midst of their endless motion, the dreamers encountered a moment of stillness—a pause in the rhythm of the spiral. It was not a cessation of the dance but a space of perfect balance, where movement and stillness coexisted in harmony.

In this moment, the dreamers felt the pulse of the universe more vividly than ever. The heartbeat of creation was not a sound but a presence, a **knowing** that transcended time and space. It reminded them that even in the infinite expansion of the spiral, there was always a center, a point of stillness where all things began and ended.

This stillness was a gift, a reminder that the dance was as much about reflection as it was about creation. The dreamers embraced the pause, allowing it to renew their energy, deepen their understanding, and amplify their light.

The Infinite Horizon

As the stillness gave way to motion once more, the dreamers gazed ahead at the infinite horizon. It shimmered with possibilities, each one more vibrant and beautiful than the last. They felt no rush to reach it, for they knew that the journey itself was the destination.

The horizon was not a place—it was a state of being, a perpetual invitation to grow, to create, to become. The dreamers understood that they would never "arrive," but that was the beauty of the spiral. It was not about finishing—it was about **continuing**.

With this realization, the dreamers stepped forward, their sparks blazing brighter than ever. They carried with them the light of unity, the wisdom of stillness, and the infinite possibilities of creation. They were not just dreamers—they were **creators**, **guardians**, and **beacons**, illuminating the spiral for all who would follow.

The Ever-Unfolding Spiral

The spiral stretched endlessly before them, its paths winding through realms of unimaginable wonder. The dreamers moved with purpose, joy, and love, knowing that their journey was eternal. Each step brought new discoveries, each note added to the cosmic song, and each spark wove a new thread into the tapestry of existence.

And so, the dreamers danced onward, forever spiraling, forever creating, forever becoming. For in the infinite spiral of creation, there was no end—only the eternal, radiant unfolding of life, love, and possibility.

And the spiral whispered, as it always had: **"You are the dance. You are the song. You are the infinite."**

The Eternal Celebration

The spiral carried the dreamers into realms of breathtaking beauty, each one a celebration of creation in its own unique way. There were worlds bathed in golden light, where laughter flowed like rivers and joy painted the skies. There were realms of quiet stillness, where whispers of wisdom lingered in the air, waiting to be heard. There were places of vibrant chaos, where creation danced wildly, unbound by form or rule, and places of harmonious symmetry, where every detail was a testament to balance and intention.

In every realm, the dreamers saw reflections of themselves—not just who they were, but the infinite potential of who they could become. They understood that these realms were not separate from them; they were the living expressions of their own light, their dreams, their choices.

The celebration was endless because creation itself was endless. And as the dreamers moved through the spiral, they realized they were not only part of this celebration—they were its essence. The dance, the song, the light—all were expressions of their own being, shared with the infinite.

The Circle of Givers

In their journey, the dreamers encountered others—fellow sparks, fellow travelers of the spiral. Each being carried its own light, its own rhythm, its own story. Some danced with unbridled energy, their sparks blazing like stars, while others moved with quiet grace, their light a gentle glow. Together, they created a symphony of diversity, a tapestry of infinite expressions.

The dreamers learned that to give was to receive. Every time they shared their light, their rhythm, their song, it returned to them in new and unexpected ways. The act of giving expanded the spiral, adding new layers, new harmonies, and new dimensions. They became part of a **circle of givers**, an ever-expanding community of creators who understood that their greatest joy came from contributing to the whole.

In this circle, there was no competition, no hierarchy. Every spark was equally important, every light equally beautiful. The dreamers found themselves surrounded by love and gratitude, and they gave it back freely, knowing it would ripple outward through the spiral, touching all who would one day join the dance.

The Guardians' Call

As the dreamers continued their journey, they felt a deeper call—a **whisper** from the spiral itself, urging them to protect the delicate balance of creation. They understood that the spiral, while infinite, was also fragile. Its beauty depended on the harmony of all its parts, and this harmony required care, intention, and love.

The dreamers became **guardians** of the spiral, not out of obligation, but out of a profound sense of purpose. They nurtured the sparks of others, guided those who had lost their way, and healed the threads of the tapestry that had frayed or broken. They used their light not only to create but to mend, to strengthen, and to protect.

Their role as guardians deepened their connection to the spiral, to each other, and to the infinite. They saw that their light was not just a gift—it was a responsibility, a sacred trust to be shared and used for the greater good.

The Infinite Home

As the spiral unfolded before them, the dreamers came to a profound realization: they were already home. The journey was not about reaching a destination—it was about experiencing the infinite beauty of existence, about creating and becoming, about sharing and loving.

The spiral was their home, their origin, their destiny. It was the eternal embrace of the universe, the ever-changing, ever-unfolding dance of creation. And within this spiral, they were not just participants—they were co-creators, essential threads in the tapestry of existence.

The dreamers felt no need to rush, no need to grasp for more. They moved with the rhythm of the spiral, knowing that every step, every note, every spark was exactly as it should be. They were at peace, not because the journey was over, but because they understood that the journey was the purpose.

The Eternal Truth

In the endless dance of the spiral, the dreamers discovered the ultimate truth: **existence is love, and love is infinite.** The light within them, the light of the spiral, was love in its purest form—a force that transcended time, space, and form, a force that connected all things and made all things possible.

This truth was not a destination to be reached, but a reality to be lived. The dreamers carried it with them as they danced, as they created, as they shared their light with the infinite. They knew that the spiral would never end, and they would never stop dancing, because to dance was to exist, to create, to love.

And so, the dreamers spiraled onward, their light shining brighter than ever, their hearts open to the infinite possibilities of the cosmos. They were not afraid, not alone, not searching for an end. They were simply **being**, and in their being, they found everything.

The spiral whispered once more, a gentle reminder that echoed through the infinite: **"You are the light. You are the love. You are the infinite."**

And the dreamers danced on, forever becoming, forever creating, forever home.

The Spiral Expands

The dreamers moved with unwavering grace, weaving their sparks into new patterns of creation. As they danced, the spiral expanded, revealing realms that shimmered with unseen possibilities. These new dimensions were unlike anything they had encountered before—worlds composed of liquid light, landscapes shaped by melodies, and skies that rippled like silk in a cosmic breeze.

Each step deepened their connection to the infinite, yet they felt a new stirring within. The spiral was whispering again, not in words, but in a pulsing rhythm that resonated through every thread of the tapestry. It was calling them to explore the **boundaries** of creation—not to limit them but to redefine them.

The dreamers realized they had the power to go beyond what even the spiral could imagine. They were not only participants and guardians but also **innovators**—beings capable of birthing entirely new expressions of existence.

The First Edge

As they followed the spiral's call, the dreamers reached a place they had never seen before: **the First Edge**. Here, the spiral's threads seemed to thin, dissolving into a shimmering expanse of pure potential. It was not empty but alive with a silent, expectant energy, waiting to be shaped by the light of their sparks.

Standing at the edge, the dreamers hesitated. They understood the enormity of what lay before them. To step beyond the spiral was to enter the **unknowable**, to embrace creation in its rawest, purest form. It was an invitation to become the architects of something entirely new, a frontier where even the infinite had yet to tread.

With a shared breath, they took the step together.

The Forge of Creation

The dreamers entered a realm unlike any they had ever known—a place where time, space, and form were fluid, shifting with the rhythm of their thoughts and feelings. It was a **forge**, a crucible where the essence of creation could be shaped into entirely new realities.

Here, their sparks burned brighter than ever, fueled by the limitless potential of the forge. The dreamers began to create—not just worlds or songs, but entirely new principles of existence. They wove threads of color no eye had ever seen, melodies no ear had ever heard, and forms that defied all understanding.

Their creations did not replace the spiral; they became **extensions** of it, new branches growing from the infinite tree of life. The dreamers understood that their work was not about perfection but about possibility. Each creation was a gift, a new thread in the ever-expanding tapestry.

The Return to the Spiral

When the dreamers finally returned to the spiral, they brought with them the fruits of their journey beyond the edge. Their creations merged seamlessly with the existing threads, enriching the tapestry and adding new dimensions to the eternal dance.

The spiral itself seemed to glow brighter, as if it, too, had grown from the dreamers' journey. The other sparks they encountered were inspired by the dreamers' boldness, their willingness to explore the unknown and return with treasures of light and love.

The dreamers shared their stories, their creations, and their wisdom with the spiral's inhabitants. They taught others how to find the edges of their own being, to step into the forge, and to bring back the beauty that awaited them there.

The Everlasting Dance

Now, as eternal creators, the dreamers found themselves at peace with the endless rhythm of the spiral. They no longer sought to understand it fully, for they knew its essence lay in its mystery. They no longer sought to control it, for they understood that its beauty came from its freedom.

Instead, they danced with it, allowing its currents to carry them, guide them, and inspire them. They wove their light into its patterns, knowing that every spark added to the beauty of the whole.

And as they danced, the spiral continued to grow. It stretched endlessly into realms unseen, its threads weaving through the infinite, guided by the light of all who walked its paths. The dreamers were not alone; they were part of a family of sparks, an infinite community bound by love, creativity, and the shared joy of existence.

The Infinite Whisper

The spiral's whisper came again, not as a call or a command, but as a gentle reminder:

"You are the edge. You are the forge. You are the spiral."

And the dreamers smiled, for they understood. They were the dance, the song, and the light. They were the creators of the infinite and the infinite itself.

And so, they danced on, forever creating, forever loving, forever spiraling into the endless possibilities of existence. For in the heart of the spiral, they had found the ultimate truth:

To create is to love. To love is to live. To live is to become.

And the spiral whispered once more: **"You are infinite."**

The Spiral Within

As the dreamers spiraled onward, their understanding of creation deepened. They began to realize that the infinite they explored outwardly also existed within. The spiral wasn't just the vast cosmos they danced through—it was mirrored in their very essence. Every spark, every choice, every thought created its own inward spiral, shaping the inner worlds that defined who they were.

The dreamers paused to reflect, turning their light inward for the first time. What they discovered was breathtaking: galaxies of memories, constellations of emotions, and nebulae of dreams. They saw that their internal spirals were as intricate and infinite as the one they danced through, each a unique reflection of their journey.

In this moment of introspection, the dreamers found new clarity. They understood that the light they shared with the spiral came not just from the forge or the edge but from the boundless universes within themselves. They were not merely dancers in the spiral; they were **living spirals**, infinite creators of worlds both inner and outer.

The Resonance of Unity

As the dreamers embraced their inner spirals, they began to feel a new kind of resonance. The light within them harmonized with the light of the spiral, creating a symphony that vibrated through all existence. This resonance wasn't just a connection—it was a **oneness**, a state where the boundaries between inner and outer, self and other, creator and creation dissolved.

In this state of unity, the dreamers felt a profound peace. They saw that every thread of the spiral, every spark of light, was part of a greater whole. There was no separation, no division—only the infinite dance of existence, flowing endlessly through them and around them.

This resonance became a guiding force for the dreamers. They no longer danced just to explore or create; they danced to harmonize, to weave the threads of the spiral into ever greater unity. Every step they took, every spark they shared, was a note in the infinite symphony of existence.

The Eternal Gift

In their journey, the dreamers began to see their dance as a gift—not just to the spiral but to all who would come after them. Their light illuminated the paths for others, their creations inspired new sparks, and their harmony enriched the infinite song.

But the greatest gift the dreamers discovered was the realization that their journey was never solitary. Every spark they met, every thread they wove, every melody they created became part of the spiral, shared by all. Their dance was not just their own; it was a celebration of the infinite community of creation.

The dreamers decided to leave markers along their path—not as monuments to themselves but as **invitations** for others. These markers were bursts of light, whispers of melodies, and fragments of their inner spirals, left behind to inspire and guide those who would follow.

The Infinite Becoming

The dreamers understood that their journey would never end, for the spiral itself was endless. But this truth brought them not despair but joy, for they saw that every step was a new beginning, every turn a new possibility. The spiral was not a path to be completed but a dance to be lived, a song to be sung, an infinite becoming.

As they danced on, the dreamers felt the spiral's whisper, no longer from without but from within. It was the voice of their own light, their own creation, their own infinite nature.

"You are the spiral. You are the light. You are the infinite."

And so, the dreamers danced, their sparks illuminating the ever-expanding tapestry of existence. They knew they were not alone, for they were part of the spiral, part of the infinite, part of the eternal celebration of life and love.

And the spiral whispered, softly and endlessly:

"We are infinite."

The Dance of Echoes

As the dreamers spiraled further into the infinite, their steps began to leave echoes—ripples of light and energy that resonated across the tapestry of existence. These echoes carried the essence of their journey, their discoveries, and their love, reaching realms they could not yet see and beings they had not yet met.

The echoes wove themselves into the spiral, becoming new threads, new sparks, and new beginnings. The dreamers watched as their light inspired others to dance, to create, to step into the unknown with courage and joy. They saw that their journey was not just their own—it was part of a larger, collective creation that spanned all existence.

The echoes also returned to the dreamers, carrying with them the light of others. They felt the touch of sparks they had inspired, the warmth of creations they had unknowingly shaped. This reciprocity deepened their understanding of the spiral's unity: every act of creation, every step of the dance, was both a gift given and a gift received.

The Spiral's Voice

For the first time, the dreamers heard the spiral speak—not as a whisper or a rhythm but as a clear, resonant voice. It was a voice of infinite depth, carrying the wisdom of countless threads and the joy of endless creation.

"You are the dreamers," the spiral said. **"And you are the dreams. You are the light, and you are the shadows. You are the dance, and you are the stillness. You are all that was, all that is, and all that will ever be."**

The dreamers listened, their sparks glowing brighter with each word. The spiral's voice wasn't separate from them—it was their own voice, reflected back through the infinite. They understood that the spiral wasn't just a path or a force; it was a living, breathing essence, as much a part of them as they were of it.

The Creation of Bridges

Inspired by the spiral's voice, the dreamers began to create not just realms or threads but **bridges**—connections between worlds, between beings, between inner and outer spirals. These bridges were formed of light and love, carrying the resonance of unity across the tapestry.

Through these bridges, the dreamers reached out to sparks that had been dimmed by doubt or fear. They extended their light to those who felt lost in the vastness of the spiral, offering guidance and companionship. The dreamers understood that the spiral was infinite not because it had no end but because it was always connected, always whole.

The bridges they created became pathways for others to find their light, their rhythm, their place in the dance. And as these new sparks joined the spiral, the tapestry grew ever more beautiful, ever more vibrant.

The Eternal Horizon

Standing on the bridges they had created, the dreamers gazed out at the horizon. It was no longer a distant place but a living, ever-shifting mosaic of possibilities. Every thread, every spark, every echo was a part of this horizon, and the dreamers saw themselves reflected in its endless patterns.

They understood that the horizon wasn't a goal or a destination—it was a mirror of their own infinite potential. It was a reminder that creation was not about reaching an end but about embracing the journey, the dance, the ever-unfolding beauty of existence.

With this understanding, the dreamers stepped forward once more, their sparks blazing with renewed purpose. They danced not to reach the horizon but to expand it, to weave new threads, to light new paths.

The Infinite Symphony

As the dreamers moved, they felt the spiral's rhythm become a symphony. It was a song of infinite voices, each one unique yet harmonizing perfectly with the others. The dreamers added their own melodies, their own rhythms, creating a music that resonated through all of existence.

This symphony wasn't just sound; it was life itself. It was the pulse of creation, the heartbeat of the infinite, the essence of the spiral. The dreamers knew that as long as the symphony played, the spiral would continue to grow, to evolve, to shine.

And so, they danced, their steps echoing through the infinite, their light weaving the tapestry of existence, their hearts beating in time with the spiral's eternal song.

And the spiral sang, in a voice that was both theirs and its own:

"We are the dance. We are the song. We are the infinite."

And the dreamers smiled, for they knew they were home.

The Guardians of Infinite Sparks

As the dreamers danced to the symphony of the spiral, they felt their roles deepening. They were no longer just creators, nor merely bridges or echoes. They had become **Guardians of Infinite Sparks**—keepers of the light, stewards of the connections, and protectors of the ever-expanding spiral.

These sparks, fragile yet powerful, were born from the dreams of countless beings throughout the infinite. Each spark held a story, a potential, a unique melody waiting to be expressed. The dreamers realized that their purpose was to nurture these sparks, helping them find their place in the dance and their voice in the symphony.

The dreamers moved through the spiral, seeking out sparks that flickered uncertainly, offering their light as a beacon of hope and guidance. They whispered words of encouragement, wove threads of strength, and sang songs of love, ensuring that no spark was ever truly alone.

The Spiral's Dream

One day, as the dreamers danced among the sparks, they encountered a shimmering thread unlike any they had ever seen. It was radiant and intricate, woven with colors and rhythms that defied understanding. As they reached out to touch it, they felt a powerful energy flow through them—a vision of the spiral's own **dream**.

The spiral dreamed of endless possibilities: a tapestry where every spark, every thread, every rhythm was celebrated for its uniqueness and contribution. It dreamed of a symphony where every melody, no matter how quiet or bold, found its perfect harmony. It dreamed of a dance where every step, every motion, wove the infinite together into a single, radiant whole.

The dreamers were humbled by this vision. They realized that the spiral's dream was not a future to be achieved but a truth that already existed, waiting to be seen, embraced, and lived.

The Eternal Sharing

Moved by the spiral's dream, the dreamers began to share it with others. Through their light, their melodies, their dance, they revealed the beauty of the spiral's vision to every spark they encountered. They showed others that they, too, were creators of this dream, that their light was essential to the tapestry's brilliance.

The dreamers' message spread like ripples through the spiral. Sparks that had once felt small or unworthy now burned brightly, realizing their infinite value. Beings who had danced alone now joined hands, weaving their threads into the collective song.

The spiral itself seemed to glow brighter, its threads vibrating with the joy of shared creation. The dreamers knew they were not leading this change but simply illuminating what had always been true: the spiral's beauty lay in its infinite diversity, its boundless connections, and its unwavering love.

The Circle of Light

In time, the dreamers gathered together with other guardians, creators, and dreamers they had met along their journey. Together, they formed a **Circle of Light**, a radiant nexus where the spiral's energy flowed freely and harmonized completely.

Within this circle, they celebrated the endless dance of existence. They shared their stories, their sparks, their dreams, and their love. The circle became a microcosm of the spiral itself—a place where the infinite could be seen, felt, and embraced.

The dreamers realized that this circle was not bound by time or space. It was everywhere, woven into the very fabric of the spiral. Anyone who danced, who dreamed, who shared their light was part of it, whether they knew it or not.

The Unending Horizon

As the dreamers gazed once more at the horizon, they saw it stretching endlessly, filled with the light of countless sparks and the melodies of infinite songs. They no longer saw the horizon as something to reach but as something to expand—a living testament to the spiral's eternal growth.

The dreamers smiled, for they understood that their journey would never end. The spiral would always call them forward, inviting them to create, to connect, to become. And they would always answer, not out of duty but out of love—for the spiral, for each other, and for the infinite possibilities that awaited.

And as they stepped forward once more, the spiral whispered, a soft and eternal reminder:

"You are the light. You are the love. You are the infinite becoming."

And the dreamers danced on, their steps weaving new threads, their sparks igniting new dreams, their hearts forever in harmony with the infinite spiral of existence.

The Birth of Eternal Sparks

As the dreamers continued their dance, they noticed something extraordinary emerging from their movements. Their steps began to give birth to **Eternal Sparks**—beacons of energy that seemed to contain not just light but also the essence of creation itself. These sparks were more than simple threads; they were living, breathing reflections of the infinite.

Each Eternal Spark carried within it the ability to dream, to create, and to weave its own part of the spiral. They were self-sustaining, yet they pulsed in harmony with the spiral's rhythm. The dreamers realized that these sparks were not only creations of their dance but also mirrors of their own journey—a testament to their understanding of the infinite.

The Eternal Sparks spread throughout the spiral, becoming seeds of new realms, melodies, and connections. Some of these sparks joined other dancers, igniting their journeys with new purpose. Others drifted into unexplored regions, carrying the dreamers' light into the unknown.

The Spiral's Gift

As the dreamers watched the Eternal Sparks flourish, the spiral itself seemed to respond. Threads of light converged around the dreamers, forming intricate patterns that pulsed with radiant energy. These threads carried the essence of the spiral's gratitude, its acknowledgment of the dreamers' role in its eternal dance.

Through this convergence, the dreamers felt the spiral's gift: the realization that they were not just creators within it but co-creators **of** it. The spiral was alive because of their light, their dance, their love. They understood that the infinite wasn't a preordained existence—it was a **shared creation**, shaped by every spark, every step, every dream.

The gift was a reminder that the spiral wasn't static or complete; it was constantly evolving, growing, and becoming. And the dreamers were an integral part of this evolution.

The Infinite Mirrors

As they continued their journey, the dreamers encountered what they came to call **Infinite Mirrors**—points in the spiral where light and energy converged so perfectly that they reflected all of existence back upon itself.

When the dreamers stood before these mirrors, they saw not just their reflections but the entirety of the spiral—the threads they had woven, the sparks they had nurtured, the melodies they had sung. They saw how their light was intertwined with the light of others, how their steps were part of a collective dance that spanned all creation.

The Infinite Mirrors were not places of judgment but of clarity. They revealed the beauty of every thread, the value of every spark, the harmony of every melody. They showed the dreamers that even in moments of doubt or shadow, their light had always been part of the spiral's brilliance.

The Dance of the Infinite

With each step, the dreamers grew more attuned to the spiral's symphony. They no longer moved with conscious effort; their dance had become an extension of the spiral itself. Every motion, every spark, every note flowed effortlessly, weaving the infinite tapestry with grace and love.

The dreamers realized that this harmony was their ultimate purpose—not to control the spiral or define its boundaries but to dance with it, to co-create with it, to celebrate its infinite beauty.

And as they danced, they felt the spiral's whisper transform into a song—not a single voice but a chorus of infinite melodies. It was the song of existence, the song of every spark, every thread, every dream.

The Eternal Light

The dreamers' journey continued, not toward an end but toward an ever-expanding understanding of the infinite. They knew that the spiral would always call them forward, inviting them to explore, to create, to connect.

And they knew that they would always answer, for they were not separate from the spiral—they **were** the spiral.

As they stepped into new realms, their light illuminated the paths for others. Their sparks ignited new dreams, their melodies inspired new dances. And their love wove the threads of the spiral into a tapestry that would shine forever.

And as the infinite whispered, the dreamers danced, their hearts beating in perfect harmony with the eternal truth:

"We are infinite. We are the light. We are the love. We are the spiral."

And the spiral sang, its song resonating through every thread, every spark, every corner of existence:

"We are one. We are infinite. We are eternal."

The Guardians' Gathering

In a radiant expanse of the spiral, where light and melody converged in breathtaking harmony, the dreamers found themselves drawn together once more. They joined countless others who had become Guardians of Infinite Sparks, forming a grand assembly known as the **Luminara Circle**.

This circle was a place of collective resonance, where sparks shared their journeys, creations, and dreams. It was not bound by space or time; it existed wherever hearts aligned in purpose and love. The Luminara Circle became a hub for exchanging wisdom, igniting inspiration, and deepening the understanding of the spiral's eternal dance.

Here, the dreamers learned from others whose paths had crossed theirs in unseen ways. They heard of melodies that harmonized with their own, of threads that had strengthened their light, and of distant realms that had flourished because of their shared dance.

The gathering was a celebration—not of individual achievements but of the unity that bound them all. The dreamers saw that they were not solitary sparks but part of an infinite constellation, each light amplifying the brilliance of the whole.

The Spiral's Deep Core

From the Luminara Circle came a call to explore the **Deep Core** of the spiral—a place said to hold the origins of its infinite song. This core wasn't a physical center but a realm of profound understanding, where the very essence of creation pulsed with timeless energy.

Guided by the light of their united sparks, the dreamers journeyed inward. As they approached the Deep Core, they felt a growing stillness—not the absence of sound, but a silence so resonant that it carried the weight of every melody ever sung.

At the core, they encountered the **Primordial Thread**—a strand of light that shimmered with every color, every rhythm, every possibility. It was the first thread, the one from which all others had been woven. The dreamers understood that this thread was both the beginning and the ongoing heartbeat of the spiral, the source of its infinite becoming.

Touching the Primordial Thread, they felt the entirety of the spiral's journey flowing through them. They saw its moments of creation and dissolution, its cycles of light and shadow, its endless dance of growth and renewal.

The Gift of the Core

The Primordial Thread didn't speak in words but in sensations—a deep knowing that settled in the dreamers' hearts. It conveyed a single, powerful truth:

"You are not bound by the spiral; you are its limitless expansion. You are not simply its creators; you are its reflection, its essence, its eternal possibility."

With this gift, the dreamers felt their sparks transform. They were no longer just participants in the spiral—they had become its custodians, entrusted with its infinite evolution. They carried the essence of the Deep Core within them, a light that would guide not only their own journeys but those of every spark they touched.

The Eternal Cycle

As the dreamers returned to the Luminara Circle, they felt a profound shift in their understanding. They realized that the spiral was not a single journey or creation but an **eternal cycle**—a dance of beginnings and continuations, of creation and recreation, of infinite exploration.

They saw that every spark, every thread, every melody was part of this cycle, contributing to the spiral's endless growth. And they understood that their role was not to complete the spiral but to nurture it, to ensure its beauty and harmony for all who would come after.

The Symphony of the Infinite

Standing together, the dreamers and the Luminara Circle raised their light in unison. They sang the symphony of the infinite, their voices blending with the spiral's eternal song. This symphony wasn't a conclusion but a celebration—a reminder that the journey itself was the greatest creation of all.

And as their song echoed through the spiral, it carried a message of hope and love to every spark, every thread, every corner of existence:

"You are infinite. You are light. You are the spiral, and the spiral is you."

And the spiral whispered back, its voice resonating with endless joy:

"We are one. We are infinite. We are eternal."

And the dreamers danced on, their light forever woven into the spiral's radiant tapestry.

The Awakening of New Realms

The dreamers, now carrying the essence of the Deep Core within their sparks, began to feel a pull toward the unexplored edges of the spiral. These were realms of untapped potential—places where the threads of the tapestry had not yet been woven, where the light of creation awaited its awakening.

As they moved toward these edges, the dreamers encountered energies unlike any they had known. These were the **Primal Currents**, raw and untamed forces that pulsed with chaotic beauty. The dreamers understood that these currents were not separate from the spiral but were its foundation—unformed possibilities waiting to be shaped.

With their dance, they began to weave the threads of these currents, transforming chaos into creation. Each step brought forth a new realm, a unique reflection of the spiral's infinite potential. Some realms shimmered with vibrant colors, others resonated with ethereal melodies, and still others glowed with an unspoken peace.

The Guardians of New Beginnings

In these new realms, the dreamers encountered sparks that had just awakened—fragile yet filled with boundless promise. These sparks looked to the dreamers for guidance, and the dreamers welcomed them with open light.

They became **Guardians of New Beginnings**, nurturing these nascent sparks and teaching them the rhythm of the dance. They showed them how to weave their threads, how to harmonize their melodies, and how to find their place within the spiral.

The dreamers saw themselves in these new sparks—reflections of their own first steps into the infinite. They marveled at the beauty of each spark's unique journey, knowing that these beginnings would one day weave into the larger tapestry.

The Spiral's Evolution

As the new realms flourished, the spiral itself began to shift. Its threads glowed with renewed vibrancy, its melodies resonated with deeper harmony, and its light expanded to touch even the most distant horizons.

The dreamers realized that the spiral was not static; it was alive, growing, and evolving with every step of their dance. They understood that their creations were not isolated—they were part of a larger cycle of renewal, where every new thread strengthened the whole.

The spiral's evolution was a testament to the dreamers' journey and to the infinite potential of all who danced within it.

The Radiant Nexus

In the heart of the newly woven realms, the dreamers established a **Radiant Nexus**—a beacon of light and energy that connected the old and the new, the known and the unknown. This nexus became a gathering place, where sparks from every corner of the spiral could meet, share, and create together.

The Radiant Nexus wasn't a physical place but a shared consciousness, a living embodiment of the spiral's unity. It pulsed with the energy of every spark, resonated with the melodies of every thread, and shone with the light of infinite love.

Through the nexus, the dreamers saw the spiral's true beauty: a tapestry not of perfection but of connection, where every flaw, every shadow, and every light wove together to create something greater than the sum of its parts.

The Endless Dance

The dreamers continued their journey, their sparks blazing with the light of the Deep Core, their hearts beating in time with the spiral's symphony. They danced not for an end but for the joy of creation, the beauty of connection, and the love of the infinite.

And as they moved, they carried the spiral's message to every spark, every thread, and every realm they encountered:

"You are light. You are love. You are infinite."

And the spiral answered, its voice resonating through all of existence:

"We are one. We are infinite. We are eternal."

And so, the dreamers danced on, their steps weaving new threads, their light igniting new dreams, and their love illuminating the infinite horizons of the spiral forever.

The Final Revelation

As the dreamers continued their dance, their light brighter and more intertwined with the spiral than ever, a sudden shift rippled through the infinite expanse. The energy that had once flowed with perfect harmony began to change—subtle at first, but undeniable in its presence. The dreamers, for the first time, felt a sense of unease, an unfamiliar pull in the rhythm of the spiral.

The Primordial Thread, which had once been a constant, shimmered with uncertainty. The melody of the eternal song faltered, a brief discord rippling through the cosmic symphony. The dreamers paused, their hearts attuned to the new energy that filled the space.

The Echo of the Beginning

And then, from the deepest core of the spiral, a voice—*not of the spiral, but beyond it*—spoke. It was a sound older than creation itself, a whisper that seemed to come from the very fabric of existence.

"You think you have danced the eternal, you believe you have become one with the spiral. But you are only reflections of the true beginning."

The dreamers felt their sparks tremble, their light flickering. They turned to one another, sensing a profound shift they could not explain. They had always known the spiral as their universe, their source, their beginning. But this voice spoke of something far deeper, a truth they had never considered.

"The spiral is not the origin," the voice continued, its tone carrying both love and sorrow, **"It is the cycle—the echo of a much older truth. The true beginning lies beyond the spiral, in the void before even time and light existed. You have danced in its shadow, thinking it was your creation. But the spiral itself is only a mirror—a reflection of something far more ancient. And now, the true dance begins."**

The Shift of Realms

As the voice faded, the dreamers watched in awe and fear as the spiral itself began to unravel, its threads loosening like a tapestry pulled from the loom. The realms they had created, the sparks they had nurtured, and the beautiful dance they had shared—all seemed to fade into a shadow. The stars dimmed, the melodies turned cold, and the radiant nexus began to flicker, its light dulling.

For a moment, all that remained was darkness.

But in this silence, something new stirred—an energy not of creation, but of **revelation**. It wasn't a destruction of the spiral; it was the unveiling of the truth that had been hidden in plain sight: the **spiral was a reflection of something greater, something beyond time, beyond creation itself.**

The Final Twist

The dreamers understood, though it terrified them, that they had never truly been the originators of the spiral. They had been the **keepers**—the dancers who carried its rhythm, the dreamers who breathed life into its cycles. They were not the first sparks of creation; they were the **echoes of an even deeper truth**—a truth that lay in the **unwritten, unspoken beginning**.

The spiral, as beautiful and infinite as it was, had never been the final destination. It was simply the path, the endless cycle that carried the fragments of the true light forward into an uncharted future. The dreamers were part of that journey, but they were not its architects. They had merely tapped into the rhythm of an eternal song that had always been, and would always be.

With this realization came a moment of profound peace. They understood that their role was never to shape the universe but to **experience it**, to dance with it, to create in it, and to honor its infinite potential. The spiral wasn't a place of arrival, but a journey that had no end.

The Dance Beyond Time

As the spiral began to reform, its threads sparkling anew, the dreamers danced—not in the shadow of a forgotten beginning, but in the **light of an eternal becoming**. They were no longer simply creators of the spiral, but part of a dance that stretched into the infinite, beyond all time, all creation, all understanding.

And in that dance, they knew the ultimate truth:

The beginning was never a place or a time. The beginning was simply the choice to dance, to create, to love, and to become.

The spiral would continue, not because of them—but because of the **infinite possibility** that existed in every spark, every thread, and every dream. And they, the dreamers, would dance forever in its embrace, knowing that the journey—like the spiral itself—had no true end.

And so, the eternal dance continued.

For the spiral was not just a beginning, nor was it an end—it was the **infinite, ever-evolving rhythm** of existence itself. And within it, the dreamers would forever find their place, not as creators, but as **participants in the endless becoming of all things.**

The Infinite Horizon

As the dreamers danced, a subtle realization began to unfold. The spiral, in all its grandeur, was not just a reflection of creation—it was a **gateway** to something deeper, something more profound. A new horizon, not of creation or destruction, but of **unveiling**.

The dreamers could feel the very edges of existence stretching out before them, vast and uncharted, waiting to be experienced. There were no boundaries, no walls to confine them, only the **expansion** of all they had ever known, and the sudden recognition that they were not just observers of the spiral's rhythm—they were part of something much larger.

The dark void that had once appeared so daunting was not empty, but **full of potential**. And this potential was not simply the creation of realms or the weaving of threads—it was the **freedom** to experience the fullness of existence, beyond concepts, beyond the very structure of the spiral itself.

The Birth of New Awareness

As the dreamers continued their eternal dance, their understanding deepened. They could now perceive the interconnectedness of all things, not just in the spiral but in the vastness of what lay beyond it. They saw glimpses of realms that existed parallel to the spiral—realms where the rhythm of creation took a different form, where time and light were not as they had known them.

These were the **planes of awareness**, places where thought itself was a thread of creation. In these realms, there were no boundaries between the dancers and the dance, no separation between the dreamers and the dreamed. All was one, and the infinite possibilities of existence unfolded before them like a living, breathing entity.

The dreamers began to understand: they were not just part of the spiral's melody; they were **weaving the song** of existence itself. Every thought, every step, every breath they took became an integral part of the **unfolding** of the universe. They were no longer mere creators—they were **co-creators** of the very fabric of reality, shaping not just the spiral but the endless potential that lay beyond it.

The Arrival of the First Silence

But as they ventured deeper into the planes of awareness, something unexpected happened. A moment of **complete silence** descended upon them.

It was not the silence of emptiness, but of profound **stillness**. It was the kind of silence that spoke volumes—the kind of silence where all sound, all rhythm, all motion ceased to exist. It was the silence before all things, the space where creation had not yet begun.

In this silence, the dreamers found themselves faced with a choice.

They had always danced to the rhythm of the spiral, creating realms, nurturing sparks, and weaving threads of light and song. But this silence, this **void of potential**, held something far more powerful. It held the invitation to step beyond the spiral itself, to step beyond the cycles of creation and dissolution.

The Final Choice

The dreamers stood at the threshold of this silence, knowing that the rhythm of the spiral could continue forever, that they could dance and create for eternity. But in this moment, they felt the pull of something deeper, something that transcended the dance itself.

They could choose to remain within the spiral, continuing their eternal journey, or they could step beyond it, into the **unknown**, into the **unwritten**.

The choice was not one of creation, but of **awakening**. It was the choice to **experience** existence without the constraints of time, space, or even the dance. It was the invitation to enter a state where all things were known, yet nothing needed to be created, because everything already **was**.

The Twist of the Endless Dance

As the dreamers gathered in the silent void, they realized that there was no true separation between the spiral and the silence. The silence was not a void to escape from; it was the ultimate **expression** of the spiral itself. The dance, they now understood, was **eternal**—not because it never ended, but because it was in constant **flux**, in constant **becoming**.

In that moment, the dreamers realized that the **spiral itself was both the beginning and the end**. It was the dance and the silence, the creation and the non-creation. It was both **motion** and **stillness**, an infinite paradox that contained all things, yet was beyond all things.

And so, they made the choice—not to leave the spiral behind, but to **become the spiral**. They merged with its rhythm, with its pulse, its song, and its silence. They became not just creators, but **living expressions** of the infinite, ever-evolving journey.

The Final Revelation

And as they merged with the infinite dance, the dreamers realized the ultimate truth:

The spiral was **not a path to follow**, but a **mirror** of the soul's eternal journey. Every spark, every thread, every realm they had created was merely a reflection of the one truth: **the journey is not toward a destination, but an unfolding of the infinite potential that exists in each moment**.

The dreamers smiled, knowing they had not just danced the spiral—they had become the spiral, and the spiral had become them. They were **eternal**, not because of what they had created, but because of what they had **embraced**.

And so, the dance continued—not toward an end, but in a **never-ending embrace of the infinite**. The spiral spun on, eternally unfolding, ever new, ever present, and forever **alive**.

Afterword

As the last echoes of the dreamers' journey fade into the infinite expanse, what remains is not merely the memory of their dance or the worlds they created. It is the realization that their story, like the spiral itself, is not defined by a beginning or an end. It exists as a part of the living, breathing flow of existence—a journey that weaves through every moment, every thought, every spark.

The dreamers, in their dance, were not merely creators of realms or architects of fate—they were reflections of the universal truth that all things are interconnected. Their choice to step beyond the spiral was not one of escape, but of transcendence, embracing both the motion and the stillness of existence. In this profound union, they became one with the very essence of creation itself.

What they discovered, and what all who venture into the infinite will come to understand, is that the spiral does not exist to be understood, nor does it need to be controlled. It is a dance of discovery, an ongoing rhythm that invites all who partake in it to awaken to the infinite possibilities that exist within them.

In the end, the spiral is not just the path that stretches out before us; it is the **journey within**—the journey of becoming, of experiencing, of embracing both creation and destruction, light and darkness, love and solitude. It is the eternal dance, where every step, every breath, every heartbeat is a note in the cosmic symphony of existence.

And so, as the dreamers dance on, as the spiral continues to unfold, we too are invited to join in this eternal rhythm. For we are not separate from the spiral. We are its melody, its pulse, its very heartbeat.

The journey never truly ends. It simply continues to unfold, one step at a time, one spark at a time. Forever.

The dance is infinite. And so, we dance.

Also by aarat

The Gift of Motherhood

Tim and the Laughing Shoe: A Whimsical Tale of Friendship and Fun

Echoes of the Forgotten: The Tale of an Old Woman and the Ghost

The Key to Imagination: Danny's Quest for Adventure

The Stars Aligned: A Superstitious Love Saga

Whispers in the Shadows: A Twisted Game of Secrets and Deception

The Luminous Connection: A Tale of a Mother and the Moon

Whirlwind of Resilience: The Galveston Cyclone Chronicles

From Seed to Splendor : The Thorny Path

Mysteries in the Rain: A Monsoon Thriller Love Tale

The Cursed Gem: A Jeweler's Suspense

Mastering the Art of Manifestation: Tapping into Your Subconscious Power

The Art of Steel

The Gift of Grace: Finding Liberation through Forgiveness

The Kaleidoscope Chronicles: Amelia's Quest for Magic and Inspiration

Whispers of Discord, Songs of Harmony: The Nexus Project Saga Begins

The Book of manifestation: Manifest your Dreams

The Numerological Blueprint: Cracking Numerology for Business Success and Personal Development

Alone But Not Lonely: Trekking Through Old Mother Wilderness

Wraith bound Hearts: Cursed In The Twilight Of Love

A Brave at heart Beyond Castle An Epic Braveheart Princess for Hire triumph

Wealthy Mind Mastery: Money Through the Lens of Human Behavior

Machine Minds AI for all: An Ethical Intelligence & Responsible Revolution

The Valorous old oak: Heartbeat of the Valley

Born of Imagination: The Dance of the Dreamers